CW00939087

TRIPI

NORMAN OHLER is an award-winning novelist and screenwriter. He is the author of *The Infiltrators* and the *New York Times* bestseller *Blitzed*, as well as the novels *Die Quotenmaschine* (the world's first hypertext novel), *Mitte* and *Stadt des Goldes* (translated into English as *Ponte City*) and the historical crime novel *Die Gleichung des Lebens*. He lives in Berlin.

'Entertaining… *Tripped* is a story of front organizations, dodgy funds, bizarre experiments, assassinations, scientists, magicians, hookers, and spies.' *The Times*

'A brilliant exposé of how Dr Albert Hofmann's epic discovery of LSD got lost in the ensuing war on drugs and the corollary, its misuse for mind-control, that hurt him personally and has hampered investigation into the potential therapeutic and spiritual benefits of the pharmaceutical.' Professor Carl Ruck, author of *The Road to Eleusis*

'Norman Ohler's fascinating study involves Nazis, the CIA, and LSD in an engaging narrative that provides a mind-altering history of "brain warfare" and exposes the Cold War psychedelic fantasies of many within the US scientific and intelligence communities. A must read for those interested in understanding the apocalyptic mindset of the nascent superpower rivalry.' Edward B. Westermann, author of *Drunk on Genocide*

'With cracking prose, Norman Ohler's *Tripped* is high-octane history writing, rich in acidic humour. You'll be in ecstasy.' Joseph Pearson, author of *My Grandfather's Knife*

'"Nazis, Big Pharma, and American special agents, oh my!" Ohler takes the reader on a journey down some of the lesser-known dark alleys of psychedelic history. From promising medical treatment to weapons of war and criminal nuisance and back again, *Tripped* recounts some of the hidden origins behind the rise and fall (and subsequent rebirth) of research into LSD and similar substances. An engrossing read, full of mystery and intrigue.' P.W. Barber, author of *Psychedelic Revolutionaries*

'Fleet-footed and propulsive… Brilliantly sifting a massive history for its ideological through lines, this is a must-read.' *Publishers Weekly* (Starred Review)

'*Tripped* is a rollicking read, lively and engaging. Ohler seems to have read everything there is to read about the history of psychedelics, blended with his own research.' *The Progressive*

TRIPPED

NAZI GERMANY, MIND CONTROL
AND THE DAWN OF THE PSYCHEDELIC AGE

NORMAN OHLER

Atlantic Books
London

10 9 8 7 6 5 4 3 2 1

A CIP catalogue record for this book is available from the British Library.

Paperback ISBN: 978 1 83895 360 7
E-book ISBN: 978 1 83895 359 1

Printed in Great Britain by Clays Ltd, Elcograf S.p.A.

Atlantic Books
An imprint of Atlantic Books Ltd
Ormond House
26–27 Boswell Street
London
WC1N 3JZ

www.atlantic-books.co.uk

Product safety EU representative: Authorised Rep Compliance Ltd., Ground Floor,
71 Lower Baggot Street, Dublin, D02 P593, Ireland. www.arccompliance.com

For my parents

CONTENTS

PART III: NARCOTIC

INTRODUCTION

IN THE LATE 1990S, INSIDE A FORMER NUCLEAR MISSILE silo in Kansas, Leonard Pickard set up what was probably the biggest LSD lab of all time. The choice of this site for such a large-scale operation seems symbolic, given that the history of the powerful substance is tightly interwoven with that of the Cold War and its arms race. On twenty-eight acres of land, behind electronically controlled gates and a hundred-ton steel door that could withstand even a nuclear attack, Pickard was alleged to have produced a kilogram of the drug per month—due to its potency, an unimaginably large amount. With it, the graduate of Harvard's Kennedy School of Government was said to have provided 95 percent of the world's supply of LSD.

On November 7, 2000, the day of the presidential election between George W. Bush and Al Gore, Pickard was inspecting the facility when he noticed that his gray Zen robe, which normally would have been carefully folded and put away, had been left carelessly in a corner.* Quickly snatching up the garment, Pickard and his partner decided to clear out of there. Though they were careful to stay under the speed limit, they soon saw flashing lights behind them. "This is

---

* Pickard had once practiced with the same Zen master as Steve Jobs—and taken the same LSD as Jobs, who credited one of his trips with the inspiration for the desktop computer.

it," Pickard radioed to his buddy, who was behind him driving the truck with the lab equipment. Pickard didn't obey the order to pull over and was pursued by officers with sirens blaring. All the while the acid chemist could think of only one thing: his wife, a Ukrainian student at UC Berkley, was nine months pregnant and would be giving birth to their daughter any day now.

When he reached a residential neighborhood, the fifty-five-year-old pulled his silver Buick over to the side of the road, pushed open the passenger door, scrambled over the seat, and leapt out of the car. An experienced long-distance runner, he shook off his pursuers and after a few miles crossed the ice-cold Big Blue River, a tributary of the Kansas River, to mask his scent from the search dogs.

In the moonlight, Pickard followed a set of train tracks, which led him to a small town with the big name of Manhattan, Kansas. Unsure whether he should try to blend in among other people or flee into the woods, he chose the latter. In the distance he heard helicopters, which searched for him with infrared scanners all through the night. He hid for hours in a concrete pipe that masked his body heat from detection, and in the morning, frozen to the bone, found a solitary farm and sought refuge in a truck parked out in the barn. At around seven o'clock the farmer's dog found him there and alerted its master with its barking. Pickard asked the man to give him a ride into town, and the farmer agreed to do so. But this was only for show: while watching television at breakfast he had seen a wanted photo of Leonard Pickard. Soon a sheriff's car was speeding their way. Again Pickard fled, running across open farmland. The police car followed him over the grain stubble, swerving as it drew ever closer to him. Finally the cop leapt out with weapon drawn and placed him under arrest. The first thing he did was to pull off Pickard's wedding ring. Two life sentences without the possibility of parole, the verdict later read.

Leonard Pickard had never raised a hand against another. He hadn't stolen anything or harassed anyone. All he'd done was manufacture a substance that half a century earlier had been considered the most promising pharmaceutical development of all time, a quality product made by the Swiss pharmaceutical company Sandoz. But in the years since then something had happened with LSD. It had been knocked off course, had been misunderstood and misused, and had fallen into the disreputable category of prohibited drugs that a United States official named Harry J. Anslinger, head of the Federal Bureau of Narcotics, had created almost singlehandedly after the Second World War. Over the years friends and supporters spoke out in support of Pickard, and in the depths of the coronavirus pandemic the unexpected occurred: a judge granted a "compassionate release," and just like that, after more than twenty years behind bars, he found himself a free man.

Leonard Pickard's unexpected release can be seen as symbolic of a broader reversal within society with regard to the treatment of LSD. Pickard, who was once judged so dangerous that the law wanted him locked away in a high-security prison for the rest of his life, now serves as a scientific advisor to a fund that targets opportunities at the intersection of psychedelics and technology, hoping to identify the pharmaceutical giants of tomorrow. He also advises international corporations and universities on the development of psychedelic medicines. Every morning from six to nine he studies the latest publications coming out of research institutions around the globe.

The early history of LSD would always have been fascinating, but in the current moment it seems especially relevant. A specter looms over the world: the specter of legalization. More and more governments are beginning to rely on scientific knowledge rather than bow to the ideological demands of the Cold War.

I myself became curious about the drug when my father, a retired judge, started to consider giving microdoses of LSD to my mother to treat her Alzheimer's disease. He had asked me why, if the drug was actually supposed to help, he couldn't just get it at the pharmacy. This launched me on my research.

The more I dug into the history, the more fascinated I became. I began to see how much of the early history of LSD was shaped by the shadow that lies over the molecule, a result of the personal connection between a Swiss pharmaceutical CEO named Arthur Stoll, a kind of unwilling forefather of psychedelics, and Richard Kuhn, the leading biochemist for the Third Reich. This relationship aided the National Socialists, who were beginning to study the use of psychedelics as potential "truth drugs"—questionable research, which, after the war, sparked the interest of the US military and its intelligence agencies in these substances.

This book is what emerged from my curiosity. In this moment when, after many decades, we are finally reconsidering the nature of our laws surrounding psychedelics, it feels more important than ever to look backward and understand how we arrived at those regulations in the first place.

The fact that the US government was introduced to LSD through Nazi research shaped much of the federal government's early attitudes around it and other psychedelics; once the Nazis elicited a potential weaponized use for LSD, the drug was never able to shake that taint. An entire class of medicines with the potential to help treat diseases that otherwise are essentially incurable was caught between the collapsing Nazi regime and the early stirrings of the Cold War and saw its early promise shattered.

In addition to LSD's militarized misconception from the Nazis, there were other areas of US drug policy influenced by the Third Reich. In fact, the eventual prohibition of all drugs, including psychedelics, can be traced back to Hitler's Germany, where the Nazi approach to banning drugs, their so-called *Rauschgiftbekämpfung* or fight against narcotics, the forerunner to the War on Drugs, also inspired US prohibition policy. Indeed it was a US narcotics control officer named Arthur Giuliani from the Federal Bureau of Narcotics, stationed in occupied Berlin after the fall of the Nazi regime, who imported much of the racist anti-drug policies back to the US. He would later reemerge to play a role in LSD's early history in America as well.

When people think of LSD, they don't think of the Nazis, and yet that unseen hand played a role in framing our laws around this class of drug and in limiting our ability to use psychedelics for medical research. Only by understanding the early history of LSD can we properly assess the current discussion around the "psychedelic renaissance," the next boom in the pharmaceutical industry. We must understand the flawed logic that limited therapeutic uses for psychedelics in the first place, because understanding the roots of that logic may, at long last, allow us to embrace fully the benefits of these drugs.

The first step to helping patients in need of psychedelic therapy—people like my mother—begins not in the present or in the future, but in the past.

Berlin, 2023

PART I

MEDICINE

1

THE ZONE

WHEN THE FEDERAL BUREAU OF NARCOTICS AGENT ARTHUR J. Giuliani took up his post as narcotics control officer in the American sector of Berlin on April 8, 1946, he was thirty-seven years old and spoke, to his credit, a bit of French and Italian, both picked up on the streets of New York, but not a word of German. The former capital of the Reich was on its knees; the wounds carved by British and American bombs on the one hand, Russian artillery fire on the other, were still everywhere present. Rubble formed an eerie streetscape where the ghosts of the past roamed, while the geopolitical conflicts of the future were already making themselves felt and the battered residents were searching for the precious commodity of normalcy. Berlin was a place gone completely out of control, a place it hardly seemed possible to regulate; only bit by bit were the women who made up the rubble crews able to clear the streets and make them passable again. Here was a blasted metropolis in which thousands of people lived in ruins, almost all of them out of work, caught in a state between exhaustion and the exciting prospect of starting life over again from scratch.

The shattered economy created a paradise for grifters and dealers. Anyone in need of the most basic necessities had to turn to the black market, where they could find anything that wasn't bolted or nailed down, from prosthetic limbs to garters. These illegal markets popped up in more than three dozen locations, East and West, each with their own mixture of suspicion, desperation, and just a hint of gold-rush atmosphere, all manifestations "of the complete despair, confusion and cynicism now reigning in Berlin," as the *Washington Daily News* reported.

Hershey bars, graham crackers, Oreos, Butterfingers, Mars bars, Jack Daniels: for consumer goods such as these, war-battered Germans were prepared to part with everything from their Leica camera to their left kidney. A Knight's Cross for a Snickers! A pocket watch for a bit of margarine. Women got dolled up and offered their bodies as goods for barter. Shady characters paced back and forth, whispering appeals to passersby, several watches on each wrist, an array of medals pinned to the inner lining of their long coats, hats tilted rakishly back on their heads and a cigarette ever dangling from their lips, assuming they could get one. Allied soldiers waved fistfuls of money that they weren't allowed to send home. A contemporary criminologist summed up the situation around him: "The phenomenon of crime in Germany has reached a level and forms unparalleled in the history of western civilisation."

What was evident everywhere was a "deprofessionalisation of criminality." In Berlin it seemed as if everyone had a secret, everyone cheated and swindled; they couldn't survive otherwise. Illicit dealings were part of the everyday life of the population at large; the underworld exerted an irresistible force of attraction on what was left of decent society. Laws were no longer respected; Hitler's rigid dictatorship was a thing of the past, and now it seemed like everything was allowed: "an environment where black market dealings are a common form of law violation." *Zapp-zarapp*, the Russian loan word for the act of "taking something from someone else with a quick, scarcely noticeable motion," had become ever present.

The four occupying powers, the United States, the Soviet Union, Great Britain, and France, had their hands full in this Berlin that was now ruled not by the Nazis but by primal instincts, by the will to survive. "Working parties" were formed among the Allies to deal with various issues, including the urgent question of regulating the drug trade, which had gotten out of control.

One problem was the enormous quantities of narcotics that had been salvaged from the stores of the defunct Wehrmacht or taken from the ruins of bombed buildings and put into circulation: Pervitin, produced by the Temmler company and containing methamphetamine; Heroin from Bayer; cocaine from the Merck company in Darmstadt, supposedly the best in the world; Eukodal, the euphoria-inducing opioid that had been Hitler's drug of choice, likewise made by Merck. With living conditions as difficult as they were, more and more people took recourse to substances to help them get through the day—or the night. Drug offenses rose by 103 percent in the first six months of 1946, compared to a rise of 57 percent in other crimes. On the black market, "enormous prices" were demanded "for smuggled drugs": 20 Reichsmarks per injection of morphine; 2,400 Reichsmarks for fifty pills of cocaine, 0.003 grams. Giuliani was troubled by these high margins, fearing that the "profits . . . could be used by the Nazi underground."

In his final letter to Washington before throwing in the towel, Giuliani's predecessor Samuel Breidenbach had compared postwar Germany to the Wild West. But the new arrival wouldn't be rattled so easily. He resolved instead to establish order and lay the groundwork for a new set of drug laws that would be in effect for all of Germany. This was a challenge that the narcotics control officer in his crisp new American military uniform was happy to take on. It didn't hurt that the War Department paid him a salary that was a fourth higher than what he would have earned in a civilian post. The conflicting interests of the different occupying powers all trying to pull Berlin in this or that direction didn't faze Giuliani too much as he went about his work. After all, *he*, being an American, was bringing peace, prosperity, and freedom—and what could be wrong with that?

Not everyone took a negative view of the chaos. The writer Hans Magnus Enzensberger was seventeen years old at the time and didn't have to go to school because there was no longer any school to go to, not yet anyway. His biographer described the shattered world as a place of learning: "Even without school we can now learn a great deal about politics and society: we learn for example that a country without a proper government can be a very pleasant thing. On the black market, you learn that capitalism always gives a chance to the resourceful. You learn that a society is something that can organize itself without central orders and guidance. In conditions of scarcity you learn a lot about people's real needs. You learn that people can be flexible, and that solemn convictions may not be as unshakeable as they seem.... In a word: in spite of hardship it is a wonderful time if you're young and curious—a brief summer of anarchy."

Even Arthur Giuliani, who set up his office at American head-quarters in Berlin-Zehlendorf, couldn't deny his fascination with the unusual circumstances: "It is utterly impossible to realize the completeness of Berlin's destruction," he wrote to Harry J. Anslinger in Washington. "Perhaps after years, a fair amount of information can be dug out of the cellars where it now lies buried under the tons of debris which once constituted the buildings above it—but that time is not yet in sight." He kept himself busy, confiscating something here, arresting someone there, and sending photos back to FBN headquarters as proof of his activities. The photos captured a pair of women's shoes with hollowed-out heels for hiding narcotics, car doors with armrests full of drugs, potatoes with their insides removed. A Hershey's cocoa tin filled with cocaine. A ladies' slip soaked in heroin solution. A book with a hole carved into its pages that in lieu of reading material offered a different kind of food for the brain.

In reality, however, such minor investigative successes had little effect. The problem was structural in nature. After the old National Socialist authorities had ceased to exist, a vacuum had opened up for the illegal dealers to exploit. How was Giuliani supposed to remedy the situation? Then one day hope arrived from an unsuspected source. He received a letter from a former Gestapo agent by the name of Werner Mittelhaus. "It is a long time my intention to write to you because I wish to tell you about the activity of the 'Reichszentrale zur Bekampfung [*sic*] von Rauschgiftvergehen' during the last years of the war." It was there, at the Reich Headquarters for Combating Narcotic Crime, that Mittelhaus had been employed, and in his accented English he voiced a wish: "I myself would like very much to work again in drug offices . . . I suppose, you will have an interest on such a work in Germany, and I would be glad, if I could cooperate in a common combat of the drug smuggle." He concluded his offer by saying, "I was never a member of the SS, only a member of the NSDAP on order of my department. The proof of my anti-Nazi positions are in my hands."

The offer presented Giuliani with an ethical problem: Would he accept help from a former Nazi, profit from his expertise, let the man tell him how to police the streets of Berlin? It was a dilemma that the other Western allies were also caught up in, whereas the Russians made no compromises on this point. Giuliani discussed the idea with Anslinger, who had no scruples about it and gave the green light from Washington. "You might check up on Mittelhaus as being possible good material for our organization." From Gestapo to FBN.

In fact, the head of the FBN admired the defunct Nazi regime for its strict policy of prohibition. "The situation in Germany . . . was entirely satisfactory," he wrote. In contrast to the chaotic Weimar Republic, the Nazis had kept their house in order. "During 1939, for instance, and as compared with 1924, this decrease [in the consumption of drugs] amounted to 25% in the case of morphine, 10% in the case of cocaine," Anslinger noted. "Thanks to the careful supervision, smuggling [was] practically impossible." Indeed, "narcotic law enforcement is believed to have been very efficient in pre-war Germany." In November 1945 Anslinger had praised the old Nazi drug laws as a model for America: These were "stricter" and had a "better constitutional basis than our own," for which reason he resolved to study the control mechanisms used in Germany and in the German-occupied countries and territories during the war. His goal: "The old and successful German opium legislation [should] become operative again as quickly as possible and be applied with the same severity as in the past."

The Nazis had made quick work of drug-users, packing them off to concentration camps—for Anslinger a welcome approach. The high-ranking American government official clearly wasn't bothered by the ideological thrust of the Nazi drug war, by its being directed against Jews, with their supposedly higher level of drug consumption. He openly acknowledged his own racism, once describing a Black informant with a racial epithet in a letter to FBN district supervisors. Another characteristic statement of Anslinger's is this one made before the US Congress: "Reefer makes darkies think they're as good as white men." It's no surprise that in Washington he was openly referred to by the nickname "Mussolini"—and not just on account of his unfortunate appearance.

For Giuliani, making contact with the ex-Gestapo agent proved difficult: By this point Mittelhaus, the former officer of the once feared Reich Main Security Office (Reichssicherheitshauptamt), which had operated under the direction of Heinrich Himmler, head of the SS, had resettled in Kiel to avoid being arrested by the Russians. The British military was stationed up there on the coast, and it, too, expressed interest in working with him.

"I spoke to the British Zonal Safety Officers, who communicated with their office at Kiel," Giuliani wrote to Anslinger. "He [Mittelhaus] will probably be re-employed by the German Criminal Police in the British Zone when he is cleared." The Brits described their catch as "undoubtedly efficient and reliable," and his connections as "amazing." Giuliani's conclusion: "The British have no intention of turning him loose, which is both understandable and reasonable, considering the personnel problem all over Germany." Also urgent was the Western Allies' belief that they required the help of former Nazi functionaries to keep German society running. Finding personnel was no easy task.

But the narcotics control officer found a solution and met instead with another former Gestapo agent, one named Ackermann, an "able, energetic, and intelligent" ex-Nazi who "was able to give [Giuliani] all the information that Mittelhaus could" have given him, including on drug smugglers and their current whereabouts. Ackermann could also provide copies of Gestapo forms for reporting narcotics offenses and instructions for Nazi drug policemen in active service. Such documents were of interest to the American, potential blueprints for forms he might use himself. At these meetings Ackermann lamented that the old Nazi law was "being distorted through diverse interpretation, and [was] losing some of its efficiency thereby." Giuliani in turn hoped that "the activities of the working party here in Berlin would tend to correct this."

The American was sorry that he couldn't put Ackermann on the payroll, but said, "I feel certain that, in our Zone, he would fall through denazification." One thing, however, seemed clear to Giuliani: The only course of action with any hope of successfully getting a handle on the unchecked drug trade in Berlin and Germany was to establish "a central operational set-up through which information on the narcotic traffic, both lawful and unlawful, [could] be channeled to a central control authority." Such an authority, similar to the former Reich Health Office (Reichsgesundheitsamt) under the Nazis, should be "national in its scope." As his predecessor Breidenbach had put it, because of "the very nature of the illicit narcotic traffic, its utter disregard of national frontiers, and its frequent efficient organization on an international scale, it is my studied opinion that no set-up short of a centralized national administration will prove effective in preventing the development of an extensive illicit narcotic traffic in Germany. Any attempt at independent control in separate zones, without a strict inspection and control of all mail, commerce and travel from zone to zone will be inadequate." Anslinger had described the urgency of adopting a centralized approach in similarly clear terms—"it is an international experience that lawless conditions in the domain of drug traffic will not stop before frontiers"—while Breidenbach outlined the stakes for the United States: "Should any extensive illicit traffic develop the United States would be one of its principal victims, regardless of the zone in which the clandestine trade might have its origin."

At this point Giuliani proposed adopting the Nazi regulations and Nazi drug laws wholesale and merely replacing German designations with their English equivalents. He put together a list:

1. "Reichsgesundheitsamt" shall mean "the Central Narcotics Office for each Zone of Occupation."
2. "Landesopiumstelle" shall mean "Opium Office of the Land or Province."

   . . .

5. "Reichsrat" shall mean "Allied Control Authority."
6. "Reichstag" shall mean the "Allied Control Authority."

Anslinger liked this approach, especially since it was to be implemented under the leadership of the United States. His plan was for Giuliani's work to have an impact that wasn't limited to Germany alone. The goal of the US's top drug enforcer was to implement a global "policy shift toward a strong policy of prohibition" by means of the newly founded United Nations. What he had in mind was nothing less than to create a regulatory framework for combating the drug trade that would be applied to the entire postwar world. Continuing the racist methods of the Nazis, who had perfected the notion of "combating narcotics" as a means of oppressing minorities, was fully consistent with his worldview. Because of the importance of its influential pharmaceutical industry before the war and its geopolitical position as a hub in the middle of Europe, Germany for Anslinger took on a key role and was meant to function as an example. If strict national controls could be successfully reintroduced between the Rhine and Oder rivers, a uniform international regulatory system would become more of a possibility. At his first appearance before the UN in December 1946 as the American delegate to the UN Commission on Narcotic Drugs, Anslinger, building on Giuliani's experiences in Berlin, presented a globally scalable, Washington-dominated approach to drug prohibition. His plan was to reshape the UN drug commission into an enforcement body that would implement repressive measures as well as a uniform anti-drug protocol binding for all countries.* What he absolutely did not want was for the commission to develop merely into a pluralistic discussion forum that would permit varying views on the potent substances. His aim wasn't easy to achieve, since not every country was on board with the idea of international prohibition—not by a long shot, and especially not those that produced a lucrative opium crop, such as Iran, Turkey, Yugoslavia, and Afghanistan.† Countries such as these soon became a thorn in Washington's side.

In Berlin, meanwhile, which according to Anslinger's plan was supposed to lead the way, the situation also proved to be a challenge, owing to the city's division into four sectors. Even if the Allies insisted that they wanted to develop a national framework for Germany,

---

* Even if Anslinger was never able to put all his radical ideas into effect, in 1961 the United Nations passed the Single Convention on Narcotic Drugs, whose goal, still today, is to fight drug abuse through coordinated international action. In this measure passed by the UN, cannabis, which Anslinger characterized as "the most violence-causing drug in the history of mankind," was for the first time declared an illegal plant throughout the world (Herer, *Hemp and the Marijuana Conspiracy,* 29).

† Anslinger also had concrete material reasons for wanting to prohibit global drug production, and especially production of opium: Back in 1939 he had arranged with the American pharmaceutical industry to stockpile a large quantity of the substance so as to be able to supply not only the US, but also its allies in the Second World War. He had channeled public and private funds to opium producers in Turkey, Iran, and India, and in 1942 instructed the American Defense Supplies Corporation to acquire all available stocks of opium in preparation for a long conflict. Ten trucks filled with close to three hundred tons of opium, guarded by FBN agents with machine guns at the ready, had driven from the ports of the East and West Coast to Fort Knox, where the United States' gold reserves are stored. There the raw material was unloaded and taken to the pharmaceutical companies, where it was turned into opiates and opioids. By 1943 the Western Allies, who used these products to treat their wounded, had become dependent on exports from the US when it came to opium derivatives, and Anslinger had secretly turned himself into the head of a global drug market—a de facto global drug czar with the backing of the American government.

each had their own interests to pursue, especially where drug policy was concerned. The British were concerned first and foremost with keeping the war-ravaged German pharmaceutical industry small, while the French in general took a lax approach. "My meeting with the Frenchman was very unsatisfactory because he knew nothing of the proposal and less of the Opium Law," Giuliani complained after a discussion with his counterpart from Paris. "I talked and talked and got no sign of intelligence from him. He was exceedingly cordial ... but it was discouraging talking in the face of ignorance."

The Russians meanwhile threw a wrench in Giuliani's plans. They downright refused to go along with the plan to adopt the Nazi approach. At meetings of the Narcotic Control Working Party, held every few weeks in Room 329 of the Allied Control Council building in Berlin's Kleistpark, every attempt by the American to get all parties to agree upon prohibition for all zones was quashed by Giuliani's counterpart with the red star on his uniform cap.

Growing ever more frustrated, Giuliani turned to Washington and sent reports of "downright sabotage on the part of the Soviets." On a personal level he got along with Major Karpov, and they often ate lunch together. "I get along well with the Soviet informally. He is a stodgy ideologist. This, I find is true of most Soviets. They hew to the line with stupefying monotony." As soon as the meetings of the "working party" commenced, it was "hard" for Giuliani "to do business with" him. Karpov, along with his colleague Major General Sidorov, regularly rejected proposals to form an anti-drug commission spanning all sectors and to strengthen laws. This led to heated debates in which "many four-letter words pass[ed], sotto voce, among the delegations on all sides." Giuliani wrote of "Irretating [sic] frustration" that was "rough on the nerves." To Washington he wrote: "It has always been apparent that the Soviet Member intended from the start to sabotage any attempt ... to achieve uniformity of application."

Utterly disgusted, Giuliani summed things up on November 14, 1946: "It was ob[v]ious that the Soviets have every intention of blocking the general proposal ... The objections of their members was based on a[n] inexplicable perversity. All of their arguments were couched in terms which can only be described as egotistics [*sic*]." At this point Anslinger asked Giuliani for "a report . . . on the situation in Germany showing what [was] happening in the four zones on narcotic control and how the program [was] deteriorating due to lack of central agency," and requested, "Also show the blocking tactics by the Russians and the fact that the Working Party is just about a washout."

Giuliani got to work and wrote the desired report from Berlin. Anslinger used it to bolster an argument he had earlier made before the UN Commission on Narcotic Drugs accusing the Soviet Union of trying to flood the West with narcotic substances in order to destabilize its democratic societies—a claim that far outpaced Giuliani's assessment.

Thus the failure to keep Berlin and Germany together and prevent the Western and Eastern sectors from drifting apart was manifested at the level of drug policy as well. Because Moscow balked, the Americans didn't succeed in implementing a unified prohibitionist policy for all four zones. The German capital still lay in ruins, and Giuliani's efforts as narcotics control officer were for naught. Summing up his work in Berlin, he sounded ambivalent: "No matter what I accomplish here, I will always recall this experience as the most unusual I have ever had." This much at least had become clear to him: If his boss Anslinger was going to wage a global war on drugs, he was going to need a lot of staying power.*

---

* And indeed he had it: Anslinger outlasted five US presidents over the course of his time in office and was, second only to his rival J. Edgar Hoover, the head of the FBI, the longest serving top-level government official in Washington. One administration after another inherited and continued his structural institutionalization of racism under the cover of a comprehensive policy of drug prohibition. Beginning in the 1930s, when the anti-drug laws that Anslinger prepared first went into effect, only to be tightened over the course of the ensuing decades, more people of color than white people have been arrested for possession of controlled substances, even though there are more white drug users. Ever of crucial importance was where the police patrolled and how hard it came down: in a word, racial profiling.

2

FROM PAINT TO MEDICINE

THE CONFLICT BETWEEN EAST AND WEST OVER DRUGS IN-
tensified when the world became aware of a new category of substances. Where before the drugs whose use and regulation posed
problems to society and sent Giuliani tramping through the rubble
of Berlin had either a stimulant or a narcotic effect, now a third class
emerged that was even more difficult to get a handle on—and would
become a source of increasing contention over the years.

Unlike amphetamines or opiates, where there seems to be a general understanding of the relationship between medical utility on
the one hand and health risks like addiction or bodily harm on the
other, this new category poses unknown challenges for doctors,
therapists, drugmakers, and lawmakers—not to mention those
who actually consume the drugs. The substances in question are
the psychedelic drugs, such as LSD and psilocybin, which at the
present moment are experiencing a renaissance and are responsible for a rise in both the stock prices of those companies that have
made them their focus and the hopes of everyone else who sees in
them a promise of relief from illnesses such as dementia, depression,
or anxiety disorders, which so far have proven scarcely treatable.
These substances also fall under the jurisdiction that Giuliani and
his boss Anslinger established, and the question of how to deal
with them has to this day caused ever-increasing conflict. Unlike
cannabis, whose global legalization is imminent, these substances

that have such a strong effect on the human mind are still bound up with taboos, the discourse dominated by fear and disinformation.

With all this as background, I stumbled upon a white paper put out by the American start-up Eleusis, which has taken on the task of "transforming psychedelics into medicines." Preliminary clinical studies conducted by Imperial College in London show that LSD activates the very receptors in the brain—known as the 5HT2A receptors—that atrophy as a result of Alzheimer's disease. When I read this, I snapped to attention. This concerned me on a personal level: My mother suffers from this aggravated form of dementia. The brain, which Alzheimer's gradually puts to sleep and ultimately kills, could—so claims the report, published in 2020—potentially be reawakened by the continual administration of low doses of LSD. Extensive studies were still necessary, but there were indications that the substance represented "a promising disease modifying therapeutic" for Alzheimer's. Neuroplasticity—the brain's ability to form connections—was demonstrably encouraged, and the neuro-inflammation that is held to be a contributing factor in dementia reduced.

The origin of the most potent variety of this new class of sub-stances, LSD itself, dates back to shortly before the end of the First World War. At that time, there was an increased demand for paint brought about by reconstruction efforts throughout Europe: Every-thing that lay in ashes and ruin was to be rebuilt and given a fresh coat. The world was supposed to shine like new, to be bright and colorful, and the times were auspicious for the chemical industry in Basel, a centrally located city that had been spared by the war, Switzerland having remained neutral. Sandoz, a paint manufacturer owned by a French-Swiss family, did good business thanks to the in-creased demand and decided to invest in a pharmaceutical branch, where the potential for growth was seen to be even greater. The leap from manufacturing paint to producing medicine was in fact a logical progression. Around the turn of the century, companies in Germany had developed chemical dyes that also found medicinal use. The substances, known as thiazines, were compounds of carbon, nitrogen, and sulfur that had sedative effects. Some dyes also had antibiotic effects; one, called trypanrot, was used to treat sleeping sickness; another, methylene blue, to treat malaria.

In any case, the decision to branch out from paint to medicine seemed economically sound: People would always get sick, especially after a world war, with its manifold long-term aftereffects. There would also be more and more people who had money to spend on medicine. The golden years of the pharmaceutical industry began, and one of its pioneers, who would become the unwilling forefather of consciousness-altering substances, was Arthur Stoll, a complex figure whom some would later call a "monster," others a benefactor and man with "community spirit."

Arthur Stoll was born in 1887 in the Swiss wine-growing village of Schinznach. At the age of twenty-two, as a student at the Eidgenös-

Richard Willstätter's Berlin laboratory, 1913, with assistant Arthur Stoll (left).

sische Technische Hochschule in Zurich, he met the scientist Richard Willstätter, one of the founders of biochemistry, who received the Nobel Prize in Chemistry for his work on plant pigments. Their meeting was a lucky break for the talented young Stoll. In 1912 he followed his mentor to the newly founded Kaiser-Wilhelm Institute for Chemistry in Berlin, where Otto Hahn also conducted his research and would later become the first to successfully split the atom. In 1916 Willstätter and Stoll moved on to Ludwig Maximilian University in Munich, where at thirty years old Stoll was named Royal Bavarian Professor by King Ludwig III, a lifetime appointment. But the overachieving Stoll was less interested in teaching and fundamental research than he was in the practical development of medicines; it wasn't academic honors that he had his eye on so much as the profits to be made in the booming drug industry.

To Willstätter's surprise his best student left him right at the triumphant moment of receiving his early professorship and went back home to Switzerland to build up the new pharmaceutical line at Sandoz—a unique, daunting task. Stoll's start-up had modest beginnings: "The laboratory, which when I took over on October 1st, 1917 was an empty room without any fixtures or furniture, had to be equipped in the most simple manner imaginable with glassware and other instruments," he later described.

What direction would he take the company in? How would he structure it in order to quickly bring a successful medication out onto the market, satisfy the investors, and justify the trust placed in him? Stoll resolved to take an unconventional path, to risk it all on one bet. He was convinced that Sandoz the paint manufacturer "would only be able to establish itself and succeed [in this] new field in the long run if [they did] pioneering work" and weren't satisfied with "imitating the competition's medicines." While other companies saw their future in synthetic chemistry, Stoll was banking on research into natural substances, decoding the world of plants in order to develop innovative medicines from natural compounds—

the kind of organic approach that he had learned from working with Willstätter and one that ran counter to the early twentieth century's faith in progress, relying, as it did, on artificial materials. But Stoll loved bold decisions.

Which still largely unstudied plant promised a return on investment within a very short amount of time? Stoll had his eye on a substance known to be tricky, one with which other chemists working in the natural realm had failed: "The pure active agents in some drugs derived from plants, like morphine, strychnine, quinine, caffeine, and many others, were already known. Still unclear, indeed fully shrouded in darkness, were the facts about the nature and the chemical composition of the active agents in ergot, which simply by virtue of its curious origin as the product of a fungus occupies a special position among medicinal drugs," Stoll described it.

Ergot is a peculiar organism, a purple, parasitic, highly toxic grain fungus. In the Middle Ages the sclerotia of *Claviceps purpurea* were feared: a hardened mass of fungal tissue that tends to infect rye crops especially. If these slightly curved, club-shaped "wolf's teeth," which grew, up to six centimeters long, in place of the kernel, weren't separated out from the grain before it was milled, bread contamination could result, spawning apocalyptic scenarios, unleashing mass psychosis and terrifying whole swaths of the countryside. Ingestion of ergot caused a disease that was known as St. Anthony's fire, characterized by a contraction of the blood vessels that resulted in the loss of fingers or toes.* At times the affliction was even confused with plague.

---

* If you walk past a field of grain at harvest time and keep your eyes open, you can still spot ergot today. In order to rule out the risk of poisoning, flour is always checked for contaminants from the grain fungus. Nevertheless, ergot poisoning is still possible, especially when unmilled organic grain is sold, unregulated, directly from farm stores. The most recent instance of ergot-contaminated cereal occurred in 1985. Interesting to note in this context is the competition between wheat and rye. The latter was historically considered the grain of the Slavs and the Goths and was regarded as of lesser value by the superpower Rome. The more finely flour could be milled, the more valuable it was considered; this had to do with, among other things, the

Eerie growths with powerful effects: ergot.

"A great scourge with swelling and blisters raged among the people and carried them off by means of a horrifying putrefaction which caused limbs to separate from the body and fall off before death set in"—so it was described in a surviving report of a mass ergot contamination that took place on the lower Rhine in 857.

The fungus also caused frightful hallucinations. The paintings of Hieronymus Bosch bear witness to such outbreaks, as does Joes van

---

smaller amount of wear on the teeth that resulted from finer flour. Rye was therefore not cultivated south of the Alps. Monasteries also contributed to the spread of the more exclusive wheat, since bread used as the host would crumble if it had been made from rye. Beer, which could be consumed without breaking fast, could be brewed from wheat meal, but not from rye. For all these reasons, wheat was valued more highly; the fact that it was more resistant to ergot infestation was yet another reason it became more established over the past centuries than rye, which even in the Middle Ages was planted almost exclusively north of the Alps. (Schmersahl, "Mutterkorn," 48.)

Craesbeeck's painting *The Temptation of Saint Anthony*: exploding skulls with nightmarish figures spilling out of them, strangely mutated insects crawling into mouths, lascivious naked hybrid creatures in bizarre landscapes, feet separated from bodies, and bizarrely contorted hands—a toxic world gone mad.

This perilous, potent substance interested Stoll. He drew on the wisdom of Basel's local hero Paracelsus, who argued that it was the dose that made the poison; nothing was inherently poisonous. And in fact, traditionally ergot was also used for medicinal purposes and was of service to those who gave it its name in German: *Mutterkorn*, "mother grain." Midwives would gather the freeloading fungus, brew a concoction from it, and administer it to women during childbirth "to prevent or stop bleeding after giving birth," or if labor was becoming too protracted. There was always danger involved, however: "The amount of active agents varies within a very broad range depending on origin, age, and how the drug is stored . . . , such that again and again fatal failures would occur that could drive doctors to despair."

It remained entirely unclear what in ergot accounted for its incredible potency. "With regard to the active agents of this strange drug," Stoll wrote in an internal report, "every scientist to that point had found something different than the one before him." Established pharmaceutical companies like Wellcome in the US had gotten nowhere with ergot. Difficulties in determining the right dose had occurred again and again; the extracted agents never remained stable enough. Severe side effects couldn't be eliminated; cases of death were recorded. After countless attempts, Wellcome's leading chemist declared with exasperation that he hadn't been able to find the principal agent.

In March 1918, Arthur Stoll managed to do what no one else had: He isolated an alkaloid in ergot that was key to its effect. He named his discovery ergotamine. His lab report is equal parts precise and effusive: "Immediately within the suctioned-off alkaline solution, and after approximately one fourth of an hour within the concentrated filtered solution, there began a crystallization of brilliant prisms and slates refracting light with extreme intensity and bordered by many domes and lateral pyramidal surfaces. In this moment, ergotamine was born, which with two molecules of crystal acetone and two molecules of water of crystallization separated quite purely from aqueous acetone for the first time, because no other ergot active agent was capable of crystallizing in the same way. Dr. Steiner [a colleague] visited me in the laboratory at that moment and marveled along with me at the crystals which shone like diamonds. We both had the impression that something beautiful had been found, but we scarcely imagined the far-reaching impact of this discovery."

Three years later ergotamine came on the market as Gynergen, a drug administered to induce contraction of the blood vessels in cases of postnatal hemorrhaging. It was soon a success, and Stoll proved himself to be a visionary who had managed to carry the high standard of his academic research over into industrial drug production. His approach, using natural materials to make new types of medicine, would prove to be trailblazing. When, in 1926, Gynergen also found use in treating migraines, there was no longer any stopping Sandoz's triumphal march. One by one, the upstart outpaced its well-established rivals Bayer, Hoechst, Schering, and Merck, which together had been known at the start of the twentieth century as the "world's pharmacy." By 1923, Stoll had risen to become the director of the company. The pharmaceutical pioneer known as "fearless" seemed to succeed in everything he did. But the biggest challenge still lay ahead.

3

AT THE ZURICH TRAIN STATION

I DECIDED TO TRAVEL TO SWITZERLAND TO DO RESEARCH AT the archive of the Sandoz company, which in 1996 had merged with Ciba-Geigy to become Novartis. I was interested in finding out why LSD, which had also come out of ergot research and which according to current scientific knowledge was so promising, had never been successfully brought out onto the market. On the way I made a stop in Zurich, for a particular reason: I wanted to get my hands on some of the stuff myself. Not that I was planning to actually take the former Sandoz product. I had simply decided to have it with me as I continued my research, as a kind of lucky charm, or maybe also as a way of being closer to the object of my investigation. In doing so I was thinking of the filmmaker Paul Schrader, who when writing the screenplay for my favorite movie, *Taxi Driver,* had kept a loaded pistol in his desk drawer to put himself in the right frame of mind.

An acquaintance of mine, Pan, lived in Zurich, and I hoped he could help me out. Pan is what is known as a "psychonaut": He takes psychedelic substances to get more joy out of life and to gain self-knowledge. When I spoke to him on the phone and let him know I wanted to meet up with him—I avoided, on account of its being illegal, the abbreviation "LSD," but I did drop hints—he said no problem and suggested we meet at the train station, at a small café just past the platforms.

It had been a few years since we'd last seen each other, and we embraced cordially. Pan's eyes were shining. "Oh, I've got some first-class product for you," he said casually. "Quality Swiss goods. It comes from Basel, from the original home of LSD. It was made just a few kilometers away from the old Sandoz lab."

"That's exactly where I'm headed later," I said, and told him about the research I was planning to do in the company's archive. Curious, I asked: "And this stuff you brought, do you know the guy who made it?"

Pan was quiet for a moment. His eyes weren't shining anymore. "I *knew* him. What I've got for you is from his last batch."

"Last batch? How come?" I asked, and took a sip of my cappuccino.

Pan glanced up, looking toward the steel framework of the station roof. "He died. In an explosion at his lab."

"What happened?" I asked, surprised. I had no idea how LSD was made, but I'd imagined the process to be calm and without danger.

"It wasn't the LSD that did him in," Pan answered. "He was also cooking up methamphetamine. The whole place went sky high."

"LSD and crystal meth in the same lab?" I was astounded. To my knowledge these two substances had nothing in common, even if they were both illegal.

"Yeah, the same one," Pan said, then reached in his fanny pack and pulled out an envelope. "Nine tabs, a hundred micrograms each." Now he was grinning again.

"How much do you want for it?"

"Don't be ridiculous, it's a gift!" Pan exclaimed with a smile. "I'm not taking any money from you for LSD!"

4

ON LOCATION:
NOVARTIS COMPANY ARCHIVE

THE ANNOUNCEMENT THAT WE WERE ARRIVING IN BASEL came over the train's loudspeakers. Because I was curious and no one was watching me, before getting off the train I briefly opened the envelope that Pan had given me. Inside was nothing more than a small orange piece of blotting paper, slightly larger than a postage stamp and divided into perforated squares. Printed in the middle was a white triangle with an *S* inside, similar to the Superman logo. Below the base, in what I took to be either a joke or an homage, was the word *SANDOZ*.

At the central station in Basel I boarded a tram, and after leaving the city center behind me I rode through a neighborhood of late-nineteenth-century villas, all fully preserved. How many of these houses had been built with the profits from the pharmaceutical industry? How many owed their ornate facades to that peculiar fungus, ergot? I got out at the Novartis Campus stop. From where I stood the German border was just a stone's throw away.

I had never done research at the archive of a company before, only in various government archives in Germany, Great Britain, and the United States. On its homepage Novartis boasted that theirs was the oldest corporate archive in Switzerland. This had a nice, confidence-inspiring ring to it, as if the place was a kind of Swiss bank of information. I imagined that Novartis had a democratic sense of itself that had led the company to take the unusual step of making its archive accessible. Since really, as a pharmaceutical giant, didn't it have every reason to shield itself from prying eyes? Apparently not: The company's intent was "to strengthen the public's trust by dealing openly with the company's history as well as to promote and encourage research on topics related to the chemical-pharmaceutical industry."

Full of expectation, I set off down the path leading to the main gate. I was looking forward to the hours that lay ahead of me. Isolated from the world, archives contain occasional surprises, harbor unexpected stories, their yellowed papers offering an opportunity to submerse oneself in bygone eras. Nowhere is one closer to the source, and even if they don't look like it from the outside, archives make me think of temples, which lends the act of visiting them a mystical air.

At the company gate I was greeted by a woman with the pretty name of Florence, who shook my hand and led me clear across the campus, which was enormous but completely empty. A tiny virus had the stock market Goliath on the run, she commented wryly—"for now at least." After walking between tall, boxy buildings, we reached a path that led to a freight elevator. Although we were in the middle of the company grounds, it was so deserted here that it seemed like she was trying to lure me into a trap.

"And the archive is really open?"

"Yes," she answered with a smile, and added in a pleasant Swiss-accented singsong. "Maybe they just forgot to shut us down, since we so rarely have people coming in and out."

We rode the freight elevator to an upper floor, squeezed past a battery of mineral water in glass bottles, and walked down a hallway with four glass-enclosed offices, in each of which someone sat with a crooked back in front of a screen and took no notice of us. Archivists, I assumed. The visitors' room was at the other end of the building, and Florence invited me to take a seat at a blindingly white Formica table. "My colleague will be with you in just a moment," she said, and added, on seeing the disappointed look on my face—I'd started to look forward to working with her—"Not to worry. You're in good hands. He knows the Sandoz files better than anyone else."

I sat there for a while and enjoyed the view out the window of Basel, the Rhine, the bridges of steel and stone. Then I stood up and walked over to the far end of the room. There against the wall stood a display case with several dozen Sandoz medication packages from years gone by. I searched in vain for Delysid, the brand name under which LSD was once distributed. Why, I wondered, of all the things out on display, was the company's most famous drug not among them? Was it because it was now illegal and no longer produced here on site? Were they ashamed of LSD? I noticed that I was no longer alone in the room and turned around. Before me stood a middle-aged man in slacks, a polo shirt, and rimless glasses. After we'd introduced ourselves, I asked him why Delysid was missing from the case.

"Because it was never a Sandoz company product," the archivist affably replied.

"But I've read," I said, "that Sandoz offered Delysid in the fifties for research purposes."

"Oh, you read a lot of things these days," he replied with a shrug. "In any case it was never on the market, on that point at least you can take my word for it. There were only sample packages for researchers and doctors. But please, have a seat. Then we can discuss what I can do for you." He gestured with a nod of his head toward the chair that Florence had offered me. "Would you like something to drink?"

I sat down. "A little sparkling water would be wonderful."

"I've never once been to Berlin," the archivist said out of nowhere after pouring me a glass. "You are from Berlin, aren't you? I've heard that it's a bit disorderly there."

"That's true," I replied, and added, because I couldn't think of anything better to say, "almost like right after the war. But on the other hand there are—or rather there were—good clubs."

"Yes, yes, I've heard that, too. So a nightlife did exist before Covid." Now he laughed in a friendly way. "So then, out with it: What brings you to us, what are you looking for?"

The question caught me flatfooted, making it clear to me how unprepared I had come to this archive, a place where you undoubtedly found out more if you knew precisely what had brought you here.

"How LSD came to be, that's what I'd like to find out," I said vaguely. "The circumstances . . . what they were looking for back then. And why it isn't on the market today. Why it ended up on the wrong track, so to speak, and suddenly wasn't a medicine anymore, but instead was considered dangerous and even banned. Even though now apparently the word is getting out that it does help people. I mean, there could potentially be billions of dollars in it . . ."

"Yes, yes." The man's eyes narrowed; he shook his head and looked away from me. "Lots of untrue things have been written on the subject."

"What do you mean by that?"

"So for now I'll just go ahead and bring you the original lab books that belonged to Dr. Hofmann, our chemist, the one who discovered the stuff," he said in lieu of a reply. "In them you can read his notes on his experiments with ergot and the moment of LSD's discovery."

"That would be a good starting point," I said, going along with it, even though I found it odd to receive such a concrete suggestion from him. Were these lab books belonging to the famous discoverer of LSD something like a display piece that they brought out to every curious researcher just to quiet them down? "Also," I added, "I'd like to get to know the structure of the archive. To look through the catalog. I'd like to get a sense of what all is there."

"Oh, that won't be necessary. Just tell me what you're interested in. Then I'll go and find it for you, assuming we have something related to it."

"That's very kind of you," I smiled at him. "But I'd still like to see how the materials are arranged so that I can put together my research plan."

"A research plan?" He took an involuntary glance down at his wristwatch. "How long are you planning to stay?"

"Well, I don't know yet," I replied. "I won't be able to say until I've had a chance to work my way into things."

"OK, well just so you understand how things stand on my end," replied the archivist, "I've got a limited amount of help here at the moment because of people being out sick. The burden rests solely on my shoulders."

I looked at him and tried to figure out what he was trying to tell me. "I certainly don't want to cause you any extra trouble," I said. "It's just that it's my first time here. I still have to learn how things work. That being the case, I'd be happy if you could fill me in. So . . . *is* there a catalog?"

"No, there is not." He gave me a serious look. "I'll go get you the lab books."

After just a short amount of time, very much as though he just had to pop over to the next room to pull them off the shelf, where they always sat waiting for this very purpose, the archivist came back with a gray cardboard box. He also handed me a pair of off-white cotton gloves. Motionless, he remained standing next to me and watched me open the box, which was held closed with a kind of flat shoe-string, and carefully take out the first of the lab books.

"Photography is not allowed, by the way," I heard him say. I looked up. He affably returned my gaze, and suddenly I realized that, of necessity, he had to regard me, the visitor to the archives, as a potential threat. After all, with every visit to the archives the materials *suffered*, simply because the papers were *touched*. Tears could occur, stains. There was also the possibility that the user might not place the materials back in the box correctly, that in the case of unbound documents they might place the pages in the wrong order—or that, in the worst-case scenario, they might swipe something.

"You can't imagine what I discovered recently," said the archivist, as if he'd read my mind. "We had a graphological assessment of Albert Hofmann. It was done when he was hired; back in the thirties they still did that kind of thing. And guess what happened: Somebody stole it! I can't find it anywhere, I even asked my coworkers to look for it themselves without me around. But still it's unaccounted for. An irreplaceable item. Probably another crazy LSD fan who couldn't contain himself." He sighed. "Sometimes I wish people would come to the archive and show an interest in something other than LSD. In any case, I would have liked to have shown you this graphological assessment."

"Yeah," I said, "that would have been nice. I might have been able to pull a quote or two from it. I'm sorry you have to deal with these archive thieves."

"You wouldn't believe how cunning some of them are, the things they come up with," said the archivist, clearly worked up about the subject. "Colleagues of mine have told me that in libraries with elaborately illustrated volumes, sometimes they'll place a moistened piece of floss on the binding between the pages, marking the spot where the expensive reproductions are. Then they'll return the volume, saying they'll be back the next day. Overnight the moisture in the floss goes to work and detaches the valuable page. The next day the thief returns and all they have to do is remove the page and smuggle it out under their shirt."

"That's horrible," I said sincerely, and looked at the archivist. In all likelihood he had people coming in here all the time, people who could be visiting his archive for dubious reasons, or in any case it wasn't clear what exactly they were up to. At the same time though he knew that there were also those who came to do serious research, and this of course was worth supporting.

"I'll be very mindful of how I handle everything," I said, and put on the cotton gloves.

5

THE MICE DON'T NOTICE A THING

CAREFULLY I OPENED THE FIRST LAB BOOK. IN 1935, THE twenty-nine-year-old Albert Hofmann picked up the research into the parasitic fungus where his boss had left off a decade earlier with the development of Gynergen. In the meantime labs in England and the US had closed the gap in ergot research and isolated the characteristic nucleus of the alkaloids contained within it, lysergic acid.

If Sandoz wanted to maintain its leading position, Hofmann argued, experiments had to continue in Basel as well. Stoll's initial response was to be skeptical when his subordinate announced his intention to intrude upon his territory and dare to try his hand with the "exceedingly sensitive, easily decomposed substances." "I must warn you of the difficulties," he said before finally giving in to Hofmann's urging, "but you are welcome to try."

Hofmann promptly ordered half a gram of ergotamine from the Sandoz storeroom. Before the material arrived, who should appear but Stoll himself, who by that point never showed his face in the lab anymore but had come to take his chemist to task: "If you wish to work with ergot alkaloids, you will have to familiarize yourself with the techniques of microchemistry. I can't have you consuming such a large amount of my expensive ergotamine for your experiments!" Stoll instructed Hofmann to forget about isolating lysergic acid and not to separate the ergotamine. But this was precisely where Hofmann saw pharmacological potential. As soon as Stoll had left

Lysergic acid (left); *LSD* (right).

the lab, the man with the strong chin ignored his boss's instructions and isolated lysergic acid. His plan was to use it as the starting material with which to form new compounds.

Hofmann's first—and biggest—success came with the production of Methergine, which left Stoll's Gynergen in the dust in terms of both intensity and duration of effect—and kicked off a lifelong rivalry between the two men. A reliable oxytocic and styptic agent, Methergine is still today administered all over the world to women giving birth.

Next up, Hofmann went searching for a relative of Coramine, which the likewise Basel-based company Ciba had successfully brought onto the market, a circulatory and respiratory stimulant whose active ingredient was nicotinic acid diethylamide. Even though the acid in the ergot alkaloids was a different one, namely lysergic acid, Hofmann was betting that it would produce a similar stimulating effect if it too was turned into diethylamide. It was a trial-and-error approach, a routine method for chemists. Most of the time, as Hofmann knew, nothing came of the countless compounds that were tested. That seemed to be the case this time as well: Hofmann synthesized lysergic acid diethylamide, the twenty-fifth compound in his experimental series, and sent the substance labeled, for that reason, LSD-25, to the pharmacy division, whose job was to test its effects. But in trials using mice the animals exhibited hardly any reaction, merely becoming somewhat restless; they weren't animated enough that observers could have noted any measurable stimulating effect. *No further evaluation*, read the assessment, and research into the compound was halted. And with that the story of LSD was essentially over.

But Hofmann refused to be satisfied with this result. He still believed in the value of the complex molecule. In 1943, five years later, he gave it another try. By this point war was raging in Europe, and resources were scarce: "There was no ether, no chloroform, no acetone, not even pure sulfuric acid," Arthur Stoll recalled. Despite these more difficult conditions, Hofmann synthesized lysergic acid diethylamide for the second time.

"This was unusual," as he wrote, "in so far as test substances, once they had been judged uninteresting by those on the pharmacological side, were as a rule dropped from the research program for good." If Hofmann's actions were unconventional, the results were something else entirely: When some of the substance inadvertently found its way into his bloodstream—whether it was through inhalation or via the eyes, skin, or mouth, he was later unable to explain—the scientist felt something unusual happening. As I read in his notes: "Last Friday, April 16th, I had to interrupt my work in the laboratory in the middle of the afternoon and leave to seek care at home, because I started to feel a strange restlessness accompanied by mild dizziness. At home I lay down and sank into a not unpleasant, intoxication-like state that was characterized by an extremely stimulated imagination. With my eyes closed (I found the daylight unpleasantly harsh), fantastical images of extraordinary plasticity and with an intense, kaleidoscope-like play of colors pressed in on me without cease."

Hofmann decided to get to the bottom of this. Three days later, on April 19, 1943, he undertook a voluntary self-experiment. This kind of approach was risky, a "mad decision," as a colleague recalled: "You didn't do such things. But he was just really stubborn." To minimize the risks, Hofmann took what he believed to be a vanishingly small dose, a mere fourth of a milligram, dissolved in water, "the smallest amount at which . . . a discernable effect was still to be expected." He would gradually increase the dose over the course of the afternoon. After half an hour he noted soberly: "At 4:50 p.m. still no trace of an effect." But increasing the dose wasn't necessary.

Just a few minutes later a massive trip began: "At 5:00 p.m. slight dizziness, restlessness, hard to concentrate on thoughts, impaired vision, laughing fits." Only with difficulty was Hofmann able to write all this down. His writing became shaky, almost illegible, so rapidly did the effects come on. Unnerved, he looked around his lab and noticed all of a sudden "the ugliness of the technical world." His colleagues in their white lab coats made an alien impression on him as they went about their "meaningless tasks." The lab instruments looked to him like "monsters," and all he wanted was to get out of there. Since he had ridden his bicycle to work that morning, a quick ride home seemed the best course of action. In a shaky voice he asked his twenty-one-year-old lab assistant, Susanne Ramstein, to come with him as a precaution, because, he said, he wasn't feeling well.

Together they left the lab and reached the bike racks. They had a seven-kilometer ride ahead of them. Hofmann swung himself up onto his bike and rode off. But no matter how desperately he pedaled, he felt like he wasn't getting anywhere—this even though the strawberry-blond, freckled Fräulein Ramstein later reported that she had a hard time catching up to him. Out they went through the Sandoz company gate and off into the suburb, then along the Rhine a ways. Spring was in the air. Soon Fräulein Ramstein, short legs notwithstanding, had valiantly caught up with her boss and helped him to keep riding and maintain his balance as they passed between the streetcars ringing their bells like mad. On they went, at the same speedy clip, till they reached the suburb of Bottmingen, Oberwiler-strasse 11, where the Hofmanns lived. Susi Ramstein, usually so care-free, started desperately calling out for the neighbors after learning that Frau Hofmann wasn't home—she and the children were at her sister's in Lucerne. The loaded chemist meanwhile couldn't manage to get his own key to fit the lock. Finally he wound up on his couch, but then immediately stood back up and went rummaging through the refrigerator, or was it called an icebox, an appliance that was pow-ered by chemical substances whose stored energy was transformed via combustion into cold. In the icebox were foodstuffs, medications, and chemicals, and, thanks to the cold, reactions and biological pro-cesses that rendered food inedible and medicines unusable proceeded more slowly. Hofmann reached for a white glass bottle, inside it a liter of milk. He drank it all in a single gulp, and then another bottle, and another, everything there was: a potential antidote to counteract symptoms of poisoning. But the strange journey continued.

"When the neighbor, Frau Dr. Ruch, appeared about five minutes later, my condition had worsened to such an extent that I could barely say what was going on anymore. Everything was bathed in the wild-est of colors, all proportions distorted. Sometimes the floor began to bulge, the walls of the room wobbled back and forth, then the whole room started spinning. Nearby objects seemed infinitely far away, faraway ones moved in very close and took on uncanny dimensions."

The face of the family doctor, Dr. Schilling, hurrying over after what seemed like an eternity but was really just a quarter of an hour later, seemed to Hofmann like that of a many-colored monster. Susi Ramstein and his neighbor of many years made no better an impression: *witches*. His own body felt metallic, and on his tongue too there was a metallic taste: "Throat dry, constricted; suffocating feeling; alter-nately dazed, then again clear cognizance of the situation, while at times, as a neutral observer standing outside of myself, I noted that I was screaming half insanely or babbling unclear nonsense."

By this point it was 6:45 p.m. He had taken the substance two and a half hours earlier, and still the effect kept growing more intense, while at the same time he perceived his own condition clearly, since his mind and his powers of observation remained unaffected. Nevertheless he was unable to stop the world around him from collapsing in on itself. Concerned, Dr. Schilling took Hofmann's pulse, while his patient now believed he had already died: "My ego was hovering somewhere in the room and saw my body lying dead on the sofa." But the family doctor noted: "Heart function normal. Heartbeat regular, heart sound clear, pulse medium-strong, breathing calm and deep, blood pressure normal."

When finally Hofmann's wife, Anita, and the children came home at around eleven p.m., his condition had improved somewhat. "The visual impairments were still pronounced. Everything seemed to wobble and the proportions were distorted, similar to the reflection on the surface of running water . . . Especially strange was how all acoustic perceptions, like the sound of a passing car, were transposed into optical sensations, such that every sound triggered a colorful image, shifting kaleidoscope-like."

Hofmann slept soundly during the night and the next day woke up normal, without a trace of a hangover. He took the day off and returned to his lab on Wednesday. There he wrote everything down, and as he did so what impressed him most about this "unfortunately somewhat dramatic self-experiment" was the revelation that, in terms of its physiological effects, lysergic acid diethylamide was clearly the "most potent substance heretofore known": the strongest stuff in the world.

Arthur Stoll and Ernst Rothlin, head of the pharmacological division at Sandoz, reacted skeptically to his description and believed that Hofmann had made a mistake in calculating the dose: "It is impossible that such a low dosage could have an effect." But the chemist hadn't made any measuring error: Unlike highly toxic substances like strychnine, nicotine, prussic acid, or the snake venom cobratoxin, which only begin to produce an effect at doses of a few milligrams, Albert Hofmann's discovery packed a much bigger wallop and was, for example, "about one thousand times stronger" than the stimulant Pervitin, which contained methamphetamine and which just a few kilometers away in Germany the Nazis were feeding to their soldiers by the ton to keep them amped up for the war.

The fact that Hofmann described his discovery as superior to the bestselling Pervitin had to have piqued the interest of his boss Stoll: What was happening in Hitler's Germany set the tone for what Sandoz did in the area of pharmaceuticals. Pervitin had made the Berlin-based Temmler company rich. Methamphetamine was an added portion of energy, perfect for a performance-oriented society, and what was the war if not a challenge requiring everyone to perform at the highest possible level? Had Hofmann stumbled upon a similarly performance-enhancing drug, but one that offered an even stronger hit? And was this discovery potentially relevant to the war effort in the same way Pervitin was?

There was no getting around it: More experiments were needed. The extreme experience of his first test didn't scare Hofmann off, and again he offered himself up as a guinea pig, setting out in search of the smallest dose at which an effect would still be noticeable. When he was called up for maneuvers with the Swiss army on September 28, 1943, the chemist in uniform took a minuscule twenty micrograms of LSD, less than a tenth of his first dose, around four o'clock in the afternoon. The sun was shining and the temperature was a pleasant 18 degrees Celsius. What Hofmann was doing was no different from what many decades later would come to be known as "microdosing."

Unlike his wild bicycle-racing mega-trip, on this mini-dose he could function properly. He ate dinner with his comrades and joined them at the pub, where he drank coffee with grappa and played "footballino and billiards." Even though from the outside he seemed normal, he nevertheless sensed a subtle change and felt "very introspective, alone with [his] own thoughts, which really [were] more images and moods without clear contours." Before going to bed a "feeling of being warm and secure in one's self" came over him.

Encouraged by these self-experiments, Hofmann now synthesized close relatives of the LSD molecule, hunting for other potent substances that affected the mind and testing them out, sometimes in lower, sometimes in higher, doses. Whether it was dihydrolysergic acid diethylamide or isolysergic acid diethylamide, substances abbreviated to LTD or DH-LTD, it was the beginning of an unusual time in the Sandoz lab, where now and again the walls would start closing in on the chemists, faces would "contort into Carnival masks," and there were fits of laughter "over the crazy condition you knew you were in," as Fräulein Ramstein, who also tested new substances, would note. Walking to the cafeteria, Albert Hofmann was sometimes "a bit wobbly on [his] feet," and he observed himself experiencing "an uncanny feeling, to no longer be normal." But at the company what he was doing was tolerated. People whispered to one another that the chemist was on the hunt for something extraordinary, and held their breath in expectation.

Outside the boxy corporate building, Florence stood leaning against the rain-gray wall, smoking. "Did you make any progress?" she asked in her Swiss singsong.

"Not really," I replied, and would have liked to smoke a cigarette myself—but I don't smoke, so I left it at that. "It was all very interesting. But I think I only got to see what everybody who comes to the archive gets to see. And there's one thing I don't understand: Why did Albert Hofmann go back and produce a substance in 1943 that he'd already given up on in 1938? It doesn't make sense."

"He himself apparently said that LSD found him, not the other way around," she replied, and stubbed her cigarette out.

"What's that supposed to mean?" I asked skeptically. "*He* synthesized the molecule. It didn't create itself."

"I've got a tip for you there," said Florence. "There's a researcher, a scholar at the University of Bern. He was here looking around for several days and was focused on that very question. I don't know if he found the answer, but if you like I can tell you how to reach him. He's an unusual guy, lives in the mountains in the nice part of the year. I could imagine him being happy to hear from you."

6

SWISS CHEESE AND ERGOT

THE VERY NEXT DAY I WAS ON THE TRAIN HEADED SOUTH. When we'd spoken on the phone, Dr. Beat Bächi had invited me, just like that, up to the Oberänzi, "up on the mountain," as he said, where he kept cattle at 1,300 meters above sea level in the shadow of the Napf, a remote mountain unknown even to many Swiss that forms the border between the Entlebuch and Emmental regions.

In Lucerne, a city on a lake with giant churches and tiny houses, I changed trains and boarded a dinky regional to Wolhusen, a sleepy village in the eastern part of the Napf mountain region. There, along with a few locals, I took a rural bus that headed straight for the forested mountainside and climbed up to ever more absurd heights. I was supposed to get off in "Holzwäge"—that was what Bächi had told me—but even after forty-five minutes we still hadn't reached the stop. By this point the last of my fellow passengers had vanished, seemingly into thin air. I was now the only one left in the rickety vehicle. Suddenly the driver called out in what to me was barely intelligible Swiss German, "Holzwäge!" and pulled over onto a turnaround on the mountain, at which point the bus slowed down and the doors sprang open with a clatter. I took this as a sign to hurry up and jump off, and in fact the bus never came to a complete stop—it just kept on puttering as it turned around and headed back down toward the valley.

I stood there at the end of the turnaround and looked at my surroundings. Not a soul in sight. There was an abandoned-looking farmhouse with a hipped roof that reached to the ground, in front of it a trail sign for hikers. A foot trail led up the mountain, switchbacks winding back and forth. The Napf was a good hour and a half away.

At some point there weren't any more trees. I saw three large parasol mushrooms growing on an overhang and wondered if I should brave the steep embankment to pick them; that way I'd have something to offer for dinner. Up on the mountain there was sure to be a stove I could fry them on. After another hour, as the sun was already inclining toward the horizon, I reached a hut, in front of which sat a giant of a man with long dark hair and a wide, dazzling grin. Dr. Beat Bächi, who didn't look like an academic, but rather more like the lead guitarist in a metal band, greeted me warmly, offered me some lemonade, and proposed we go for a walk.

"LSD of course became famous as a hippie drug," he said, launching into his lecture as we walked across the flower- and herb-covered meadow in the direction of the Napf's summit, "a substance that people used to think new thoughts, no? To develop alternative ways of living, escape postwar society with its philistinism, its old-fashioned gender roles and loyal service to the system. LSD was used to rediscover the magic that modernity, with its sober forms of reproduction, had banished from everyday life. The hippies imagined, and many artists did too, that the drug facilitated the creative process, and they took it in order to get high and overcome limits, to become one with nature and the universe. The irony is, though, that the origin of this substance has nothing to do with rejecting society or anything mystical. In my view as well the thing Albert Hofmann said about it being a kind of fate that led him to bring LSD back from oblivion and synthesize it again after five years is pure self-stylization."

We had reached the end of the meadow. Ahead of us the land fell sharply downward. The world stretched out into rolling hills as far as the eye could see, rising finally to meet a jagged alpine panorama on the horizon. "There below us lies the Emmental," said Dr. Bächi, who by then had asked me to call him Beat. "Between 1938 and 1943, something extraordinary went on down there. And *that's* why we have LSD today."

"Because of the Emmental?" I asked in disbelief.

"They made more down there than cheese with holes in it," Beat replied.

7

AGROCHEMISTRY

THANKS TO THE TRIUMPHANT SUCCESS OF ALBERT HOF-
mann's Methergine, sales of ergot products rose precipitously
at Sandoz. The company brought more and more drugs onto the
market that were based on the alkaloids of the grain fungus: hydergine for treating impaired circulation in the extremities as
well as impaired brain function in old age; Cafergot and Deseril
for migraines; dihydroergotamine for treating headaches, shingles,
and trigeminal neuralgia; Bellergal, a sleep medicine and sedative;
Parlodel for treating Parkinson's disease. All these were fruits of
the natural chemical lab in which Albert Hofmann plied his trade:
medicines that over the years brought hundreds of millions into
the company's coffers.

These mounting successes led to a problem: Ever larger quantities
of ergot were needed. The method used up to this point of gathering ergot in the wild in Spain and Portugal was labor-intensive and
costly, with minimal yields.

"In the late thirties, in order to have more ergot at their disposal,
Sandoz changed their approach," Beat explained as we left his hut
ever farther behind us. "And the Emmental played the key role. Do
you see the fog among the hills over there? It's difficult terrain for
farming. The slopes are steep, the arable land scarce, with plots often less than half an acre. There's a lot of shade. In the morning the
dew lies heavy on the grain and in the evening there's this stubborn

fog. A poor region, Protestant. Child labor was always a fact of life here. Subsistence wasn't possible without it. But here, of all places— such was the thinking at Sandoz—here it might just be possible: large-scale cultivation of the valuable toxin. The reason being that because of the damp climate, the grain is frequently infested with ergot naturally anyway. If we pick up the pace a little, I can show you one of the old fields before sundown."

The delegation from Basel opened what they called the ergot office in the late 1930s in a tiny town named Weiher. The man chosen to run it, a passionate hunter by the name of Max Schori, promptly began racing around the region in his Jaguar, always carrying with him a pistol and his hunting dog. He had to convince local residents to go along with the plan to cease cultivation of the nourishing grain and instead grow the hated ergot, which for centuries they had avoided and despised. Obviously this wasn't easy: "First and foremost, the fearfulness of the farmers and their negative attitude toward anything new must be taken into account," a letter sent to Arthur Stoll from the Emmental put it.

The locals feared that ergot cultivation would bring disaster. They worried it would contaminate the soil over the long term if the fungus were carried by the wind and landed on the soil. Sandoz's refusal to take responsibility for potential damages in neighboring fields didn't inspire confidence. And there was yet another reason why the pharma company's plans were hard for the farmers to swallow: In 1940, as the Second World War seized the entire continent in its grip, the Swiss Confederation had declared the so-called Anbauschlacht—"cultivation battle"—which required all Swiss food producers to increase their output of foodstuffs. The War Nutrition Office (Kriegsernährungsamt) in Bern had to agree to Sandoz's plan and recognized the "great national economic significance" of ergot. The fungus was judged to be of greater importance than the crop shortfalls in grain production. On top of that, Stoll had an argument ready that finally changed the minds of the region's farmers: "The factory," as he called Sandoz, would pay up to twenty francs per kilogram of ergot, several times the price of rye.

The transition to grain fungus production changed everything in the backwoods of the Emmental. What Sandoz accomplished here was nothing less than an agrochemical revolution, the ramifications of which extended beyond just Switzerland. This was, at the time, the most significant growing operation of medicinal plants to date in central Europe. Thanks to the chemistry experts from Basel, the good old farmer transformed into a supplier for the pharmaceutical industry, a link in a chain of exploitation.

Most astounding for the growers was that the company itself supplied the seeds for the grain that was to be infested with ergot. The seeds in question were of Kluser Roggen Spezial—special Kluser rye—developed especially for the purpose at Sandoz's agricultural research station, the Klus Hof.

With its long ears and strong stalks, it was tailor-made for a high-yield fungus infestation. The pharmaceutical concern had even put in patent claims, a novelty at the time, and the farmers weren't permitted to use the seeds for any other purpose, much less sell them. They had to obtain the seeds directly from Sandoz; otherwise they were barred from participating in the lucrative cultivation program. The businesspeople from the city even supervised the application of fertilizer: A Sandoz-produced phosphor fertilizer was recommended, as were the pesticide Extar and the insecticide Sandolin, also made by Sandoz, plus, finally, Kupfer Sandoz, this too for fighting pests.

First the locals had to learn how to inoculate. Ergot was only profitable when it was cultivated on a grand scale resulting in a "reliable mass infection." Young Emmentaler girls with their blond hair in braids were armed with inoculation guns and sent off into the fields to shoot the mycelium into the floral buds of the grain. The substance used for inoculation was a white powder that the Sandoz men brought in briefcases, not saying anything about the composition of what they brought. There were eight active "section managers" dispatched from headquarters, thirty-four "machine auxiliaries," three

Inoculating with inoculation gun.

people for "technical machine supervision," thirty-one inoculation machines. Sixteen Jeeps and several motorcycles wound their way up and down the switchbacks, and fifteen ergot tractors with Sandoz pennants and round goggle-eyed headlights were driven on the slopes by specially engaged "machine managers."

"All of this worked to ensure that the standardized high-yield variety grew optimally and produced the maximum yield, no matter how steep the slope or what the composition of the soil was," said Beat as we trudged farther downhill and reached the field that he wanted to show me. It wasn't large, maybe a quarter of an acre, and lay before us black as night. Rye was growing in it, tall, over our heads. I grabbed one of the stalks and, when running my hand along its length, sliced my palm open on the sharp edge. I jerked my hand back. For a moment I stared at it in surprise: a fine red line was starting to show.

"Picking ergot was endless and monotonous," I heard Beat saying. "But for Sandoz the gigantic undertaking was a success. In the early forties, all over the Emmental, as well as on the other side of the Napf, in the backcountry outside of Lucerne, they achieved consistent results. In the village of Trub they celebrated the autumn toxin haul. Sandoz treated everyone to a ceremonial post-harvest beer and a hearty *Ratsherrentopf* stew at the pub. Once a year the farmers got to feel like big men, but at five p.m. sharp the party was over and it was back to their families on the farm. Then the Sandoz freight cars rolled off, and in Basel the storeroom filled with ergot, ready for the natural chemists working with Albert Hofmann to extract the alkaloids."

Beat came to his conclusion as we scrambled back up to his hut: "For Sandoz the high-tech intervention in the Emmental meant their entry into agrochemistry and biotechnology. The notion of owning property rights in biological organisms was completely transformed. Ergot meant maximized-profit agriculture with complete disregard for depleted soil. It was the beginning of the systematic use of fertilizer and pesticide, of large-scale spraying, the opposite of sustainable, organic farming. In this regard as well it had nothing to do with the hippie ideals that came to be associated with LSD in the sixties. In 1943 Albert Hofmann produced this substance again not out of intuition, not because he was unconsciously following some kind of fate, as he later claimed, but because his company needed new products."

For dinner there were brown bratwursts in an onion sauce and the parasol mushrooms I'd foraged, plus *knöpfli* to go with it. We drank a few glasses of plum brandy, and soon it was night. I couldn't sleep yet. Beat had hung a hammock between two two-hundred-year-old ash trees overlooking the meadow outside, their branches soaring up into the starry sky. There I now lay. I felt good, felt the cozy sensation of my belly sinking down toward the earth's center, while my mind went in the opposite direction and I thought back over what Beat had said: that LSD hadn't come from heaven, but rather was the result of a pharmaceutical company's sober efforts to develop new medicines, a company that wanted to process the raw material, ergot, that it had gone to such lengths to obtain.

What market did the company have in mind in 1943? Where did Arthur Stoll see the largest potential profit margins? Suddenly I realized that I needed to see *his* papers, not just Hofmann's, who as a chemist was certainly active in the lab, but didn't determine the direction of drug development. I had to go back to the Sandoz archive.

Early the next morning I accompanied Beat out onto the wide meadow to milk the cows. We joked about the idiosyncrasies of the region, while within me the anticipation grew and I looked forward to going back to Basel. Back at the hut I packed my bag, looked up the next train connection, and said goodbye. Before leaving I checked my email again.

Dear Herr Ohler,

Currently I'm on my own here at the archive (people out on vacation, out sick, part-time work quotas met). On top of that, I have to leave the archive at 3:45 today. Please don't be angry with me if I must ask you to put off your visit.

Warm regards,
Novartis International AG

After discussing the situation with Beat, I decided to act as though I hadn't seen the archivist's email in time. I shouldered my backpack and plodded off. After an hour and a half I was back in the old bus, this time headed down the mountain. Again I asked myself: What medications were in demand in 1943? Possibly those that were bound up with the all-consuming war.

During the train ride to Basel I started researching the Swiss economy during World War II. I came across a document that investigated the role that companies played in the country's collaboration with the Nazi regime. What I'd found was the *Final Report of the Independent Commission of Experts Switzerland—Second World War*, authored by forty historians, which the government in Bern had commissioned in 1996. Clearly there was a fair amount to sort through; the text ran to a full 525 pages, not counting notes. In their report, the authors shed light on the role played by banks, insurance firms, and other companies, detailing gold transactions, illegal arms deals, "aryanizations," and exploitation of forced laborers by Swiss companies in Germany and territories occupied by the Wehrmacht.

The introduction laid out the reason for such an exhaustive report: True, Switzerland had remained neutral during the Second World War. But the historical reality, the authors wrote, was more complex, given that between 1940 and 1944 the country was surrounded on all sides by the Axis powers. "The entire policy . . . will consist in playing for time," as one Swiss politician quoted in the report said in 1943; characteristic of this stance was an effort not to ostracize Nazi Germany in any way and not to explicitly take the side of the Allies. Switzerland made no judgments, it merely observed what was happening from its "balcony." Because the standard of living of the country's population depended on its economic ties to its fascist neighbors Germany and Italy, as well as occupied France, which was cooperating with the Nazis, revenue from trade with the Axis actually increased after 1940, when Hitler began to extend his victory march throughout Europe.

Nazi Germany and the Swiss Confederation profited from each other. Switzerland had a stable, convertible currency that was attractive to the Third Reich, which was chronically in need of foreign currency. The Swiss National Bank shamelessly bought the murdering brownshirts' plundered gold off of them; private manufacturers like Oerlikor-Bührle and even state-owned producers fulfilled substantial arms shipment orders. The country's train and road networks continued to function and offered the quickest connection between Germany and its closest ally, Italy. German-speaking Switzerland continued to have close cultural and personal ties to its large neighbor to the north. People knew each other. The personal network between Germans and Swiss Germans continued to exist, unimpeded, throughout the war. Neutrality was treated as a relative concept.

But where did the legitimate efforts of an encircled country to procure existentially important goods like coal, iron, food, and seeds end, and where did the lucrative business of war profiteers, who kept up trade with the fascist regime through the spring of 1945, begin? These loyalties were a thorn in the Allies' side: Switzerland was "an economic satellite of the Axis, and the source of part of Axis economic and military power"; the Confederation maintained "economic integration without political participation." As a standard joke of those days had it, all those who, following Switzerland's partial *de*mobilization in 1940, went back to the office or the factory worked six days a week for the Germans and on the seventh day prayed for Allied victory.

What did Arthur Stoll do?

8

LSD IN THE ARCHIVE

"YES, GOOD MORNING, SO YOU CAME ANYWAY" WERE THE words with which I was greeted. I had walked down the hallway into the visitors' room, sat down at the Formica table, and was looking out through the window. Next to me stood the archivist, staring at me with a look of astonishment.

"I did ask you to contact me in advance and let me know what you'd like to see by email so that I could have everything ready," he said in his affable voice. "I'm sorry to say it but I really don't have any time for you today. So then, what do we do now?"

I thought for a moment. My gaze landed on the Basel city center, untouched by the war, everything intact. Had Switzerland been spared by the Wehrmacht, which had brought devastation to every other country in Europe, because the Swiss had eagerly cooperated with the National Socialists?

"But now I know exactly what I'd like to see," I said finally.

"That may well be, but as I've told you I've got an incredible amount of work piled up on my desk today and have to leave early. The only thing I could give you at short notice would be the correspondence between Albert Hofmann and Aldous Huxley. The latter was very active on the LSD front very early on, you know. That should be of interest to you as a writer. I pulled the letters from the collection especially for you the last time you were here, but you weren't able to get to them." Before I could protest, the archivist took a light gray box from the metal cart that he used to shuttle materials from here to there. "So unfortunately I now have to get back to my own work," he said, and placed the box on the table in front of me. And just like that he was gone.

I let out a sigh and poured myself a glass of water. Listlessly I opened the first folder and looked at the handwritten letters from the fifties that the author of *Brave New World* had exchanged with the man who discovered LSD. Both men affirmed to each other their belief that LSD could be of use in psychotherapy and self-discovery, though Hofmann wanted to restrict use of the powerful substance to a cultural elite: intellectuals, artists, scientists, and others of that ilk. He couldn't imagine use on a mass scale.

Huxley proposed a meeting at a conference in Rome, where together they could "[learn] more about this new door into the other world of the mind." At that time the writer was the most prominent voice speaking out in favor of psychoactive substances. In his essays "Heaven and Hell" and "The Doors of Perception"—from which the rock band the Doors would later get their name—he had described how under the influence of such substances a valve had opened up in his brain and he was inundated with a wave of intense impressions, whereas by contrast the sober state admitted only a trickle of perceptions. Huxley's publications had aroused great interest and led to massive uptick in research, both scientific and at the level of popular culture—but at the moment I wasn't interested in any of this. Instead I wanted to know what had happened with LSD *before* then, in the latter half of the *forties*, when Giuliani was patrolling Berlin and Anslinger was paving the way for a global prohibition of drugs. Why had LSD also ended up subject to state restrictions rather than being brought out onto the market as a therapeutic?

How could I get the archivist to find and bring out what I really wanted to see? Suddenly I had to pee. I stood up restlessly and walked down the hall a ways until I spotted a sign that pointed me in the direction of the toilets, straight into the archive itself, the room where the documents were stored. I was surprised that they would let me walk through these hallowed halls unsupervised. Here, in countless gleaming steel cabinets, the materials were stowed away. Large three-armed handles, a black ball on the end of each arm, begged to be turned, but since I had no idea where anything was—and definitely not where Stoll's correspondence was kept—an unauthorized search was out of the question. For a moment my gaze lingered on the rear wall of the long room. Hanging there was an old Sandoz flag, its dark orange color reflected in the polished metal doors of the document cases. Suddenly I got an idea. After I had relieved myself, I walked down the hall past the glass-walled offices, back toward the visitors' room. The door to the archivist's office was open, and I stepped inside. There he sat behind his desk. He raised his head and looked at me.

"Do you also have LSD here, in the archive?" I asked abruptly.

"Come again? What do you mean?"

"Like, actual LSD," I explained. "The former Sandoz product."

"It was never an official product, we've been over this already," he replied, and added, "But leaving that aside: No, I've never laid eyes on LSD. After all, they stopped making it."

"Not on the black market," I said. "Would you like to see it?"

He shrugged. "Why not? But I wouldn't know how or where."

"I've got some with me," I said, and took the envelope Pan had given me out of my jacket pocket. I brought out the tiny square with the dark orange design and set it down in front of the archivist.

"Huh?" he asked, staggered. "But . . . but that's the old Sandoz logo!"

"It might be meant as an homage," I said. "In any case, this stuff was made here in Basel."

"Well, this is all very interesting," replied the archivist, still staring at the LSD. "But this is just a piece of blotting paper!"

"Exactly!" I cried. "That's what my book is about: why it's not in a Sandoz box, or now rather a Novartis box. In a dropper bottle, for example. It does have medical uses—your company determined that to be one hundred percent the case back when the product was first being developed. If my information is correct, there wasn't a single clinical study that found harmful effects or the risk of dependency."

"Oh, that's all beyond me," said the archivist.

"Would you like some?"

He looked at me, confused.

"There in front of you are nine trips," I explained. "They were given to me, and I would be very happy to pass one of them along to you. As a token of my gratitude for your help, despite my showing up unexpectedly today."

"A gift?" He paused, taken aback, and sat up straighter. "You would do that? Oh, but I couldn't accept this."

"Why not?" I said encouragingly. "I mean, LSD was discovered here on this campus by a Sandoz employee, a former colleague of yours, so to speak. It's still the same exact molecule that your company once produced."

"Well, sure, that's true," he said hesitantly.

"You could also archive it."

Now he laughed.

"Probably best to keep it in the refrigerator," I merrily continued, and detached one of the squares from the sheet, the one in the bottom right corner. Then with some ceremony I handed it to the archivist, who received it almost reverently.

"Well, yes, thank you very much," he said, his whole face beaming. He seemed to be truly happy about it. Possibly there was a touch of pride showing through, the hidden, repressed pride that those who worked at Sandoz felt for their most famous, albeit so anathematized, product.

"But . . . ?" He wasn't exactly sure how to put the question.

"If you want to try it out, I would recommend being out in nature," I said. "While out hiking, for example, on a nice day. I heard once that that's what Albert Hofmann recommended."

"Oh okay," the archivist said, and nodded. "I just swallow this little piece of paper? Or do I lick it?"

"Pop it in your mouth and down the hatch," I said. "And please, write me an email: Tell me what your experience was like. I'd be interested to know."

"That's considerate of you." The archivist looked out the window and thought for a moment. "But I think that given the legal situation, I just have to decline." He handed the paper square back to me.

"No problem," I said, and took it back.

"Thank you anyway for the generous offer. Can I at least show my appreciation in some way?"

"No need," I replied. "You've been a big help already."

"Is there anything else in the archive," he insisted, "that you'd still be interested in seeing today?"

"Well, to be honest . . . But do you have time?"

"It depends what you'd like to see. What did you have in mind?"

"The correspondence of Arthur Stoll from 1938 into the early postwar years."

"Oh, Arthur Stoll? That's no problem," said the archivist, standing up from his swivel chair. "I'll get it for you right away."

9

ARTHUR STOLL'S ART

AFTER A FEW MINUTES HAD PASSED THE ARCHIVIST CAME back to my table pushing the little metal cart. "So, here you have the correspondence of our long-serving supervisory board president, Professor Arthur Stoll," he said somewhat bombastically. "It was really no problem at all to go track this down for you. If all your requests are this simple, it won't tie up anybody here." He gave me a friendly smile and withdrew, saying he would leave me alone now; he had things to do.

Excited, I opened the first of the gray binders, took out the topmost of the beige envelopes, and undid the string that held it closed. Inside lay letter after letter of neatly compiled correspondence, typewritten for the most part, with the occasional handwritten letter mixed in. A few of the papers were over one hundred years old.

It didn't take long for it to become clear that Stoll had kept up a particularly intense communication with his mentor, Richard Willstätter, winner of the Nobel Prize in Chemistry. But there was one more person with whom countless letters had been exchanged. This person's name was also Richard, his last name Kuhn: a German scientist who would come to be one of the twentieth century's most significant chemists, and who after Stoll's departure for Sandoz took his place as their old professor Willstätter's new protégé.

Kuhn and Stoll developed a decades-long collaborative relationship, which they maintained in "strict confidence." They exchanged information and helped each other out, each on his own side of the border. Going back as far as the days of the Weimar Republic, Kuhn frequently traveled to Basel and took part in Stoll's ergot research. Stoll even held out the prospect of a share in the profits, which ordinarily he was not at all willing to grant: If Sandoz were to develop products that were based on Kuhn's contributions, "then an appropriate share of the earnings should . . . be rendered to the laboratory of Herr Prof. Kuhn . . . The Sandoz company would be . . . prepared to render appropriate compensation for the experiments and if appropriate to hand the field of inquiry over to the laboratory of Herr Prof. Kuhn for further investigation." Thus Sandoz became a kind of second lab for the youthful-looking Richard Kuhn, with his wild shock of red-brown hair and crafty smile—and his lab in Germany an off-site research station for Arthur Stoll.

I worked through one folder after another, while the years in the headings of the letters moved ever closer to 1933. How did this friendship and scientific collaboration shift after the situation in Germany radically changed? Willstätter, their "most cherished teacher," was a Jew, Kuhn an "Aryan," and Stoll Swiss. In July of that year, which for Germany—and the rest of the world as well—signified the beginning of a disastrous new era, Willstätter was presented with the prestigious Willard Gibbs Award in the United States, honoring him as one of the world's leading scientists in organic chemistry. In Nazi Germany, on the other hand, the Nobel laureate was barred from teaching.

Neither were Jews in Germany particularly welcome in leading positions in business anymore, either. Since 1930, Willstätter had served, at Stoll's request, as the chairman of the supervisory board of the Sandoz branch in Nuremberg. But in 1933, when the National Socialist government suggested to all foreign companies that they "voluntarily" part ways with their "non-Aryan" employees, the Swiss executive immediately caved and removed his mentor Willstätter from the Nuremberg board. Their relationship cooled: Stoll had responded all too eagerly to the wishes of the fascist powers

that be, even though the director of the Nuremberg office, Fritz Aus-
berger, had pointed out to him "that what was being demanded was
not the complete elimination of all Jews and foreigners from advisory boards under all circumstances." Whereas other Basel chemical
firms, such as Hoffmann-La Roche, didn't capitulate so quickly and
kept their managers in Germany into the year 1938, Sandoz hurried
to please the Nazis, increasing share capital in order to reduce the
share of Swiss investment and lend the Nuremberg branch office
at Deutschherrenstrasse 15 a more Germanic character. Stoll's personal ties to Willstätter, to whom he owed so much, clearly mattered
less to the Swiss executive than commercial interests.

It got worse. Stoll had no scruples about doing business with the
unjust system even after receiving detailed reports of the monstrous
acts committed by the National Socialists, such as, in 1942, the so-
called euthanasia program T4, over the course of which more than
two hundred thousand people with physical, mental, or psychological disabilities were murdered—the "extermination of life unworthy
of living," as it was known in cynical Nazi jargon. The expert report
commissioned by the Swiss government confirms, "In 1942 Sandoz
was fully informed about the 'euthanasia' programme, i.e., the murder
of handicapped people." A common method of execution was an
overdose of morphine, though it is still today unclear who the suppliers were. In part it came from the Reich Headquarters for Combating Narcotic Crime in Berlin, the authority for which Giuliani's
contact Werner Mittelhaus had worked. But it has been proven that
Sandoz also supplied opiates to the mass murderers.

Just as Switzerland as a whole had done, Stoll profited from the
criminal policies of the Nazi system, including the exclusion from
society of Willstätter and other Jews in Germany. This was true on
a personal level as well: The pharma boss used his former mentor as
a go-between for purchasing artworks that his Jewish friends were
forced to sell to make ends meet. Stoll had taken a particular liking
to Ferdinand Hodler, Switzerland's most famous artist: "Dear friend
Willstätter," he wrote on August 20, 1935, "You mentioned briefly

that paintings by Ferdinand Hodler in Germany are going down in price. You know that I dearly love Hodler paintings, and I would like to let you know, just in case, that given a favorable opportunity I wouldn't be disinclined to purchase individual good paintings by Ferdinand Hodler, if you hear of anything to that effect among your circle of acquaintances."

Buying up art from the German Reich, where prices for works owned by Jews were tumbling, remained attractive to Stoll for years. "I'm glad that you have purchased the painting depicting the Dutch harbor by night for me, and ask that you let me know which account I should deposit the sum in via the German-Swiss clearing house," he wrote to Willstätter in December 1938. The work in question was Eduard Schleich the Elder's *Holländische Flusslandschaft mit Mühle bei Mondschein*. The stated purchase price was five hundred Swiss francs, a small sum. In his memoirs Willstätter writes about what was happening in Munich, where he lived: "Towards the end of 1938, when I was preparing to emigrate, the buying up of artworks from non-Aryan homes via intermediaries was in full swing. There were middlemen whose aim was to enrich themselves."

A number of valuable artworks found their way to Basel, where Stoll took advantage of the favorable times to build up his art collection. Soon he possessed the largest collection of Ferdinand Hodler's paintings in the world, with over one hundred, and had sculptures by Rodin to call his own, as well as paintings by Cézanne, Van Gogh, Munch, Liebermann, Corinth, and many others.*

---

* In 1961 Stoll financed an extensive "Special Commissioned Publication" produced by the Swiss Institute for Art Research: *Sammlung Arthur Stoll—Skulpturen und Gemälden des 19. und 20. Jahrhunderts* (Arthur Stoll Collection—Sculptures and Paintings from the 19th and 20th Centuries). As the introduction to the volume, sumptuously illustrated with 44 color panels and 376 reproductions, proclaims: "Not all museum directors and private collectors, who eagerly hoard treasures, recognize and fulfill the moral obligation that is inseparably bound up with the ownership of artworks. For Arthur Stoll it is self-evident." (Brüschweiler, Diggelmann, and Lüthy, *Sammlung Arthur Stoll*)

But what became of Richard Willstätter in these years in which the Nazis enriched those industry bosses who chose to play along? The Jewish scientist had to give up his career, and devoted himself thenceforth to growing roses at his home in the Munich neighborhood of Bogenhausen. The flowers were what saved him after the November pogrom in 1938, when the Gestapo paid a visit to his house intending to pack him off to a concentration camp. The agents didn't find Willstätter in the house and neglected to search the garden, where the Nobel laureate was hiding among his beloved plants. The mortal danger he was in had suddenly become real, and "to travel abroad difficult." In an act of desperation Willstätter attempted to flee to Switzerland across Lake Constance in a rowboat and was arrested. Now Stoll stepped into action, assuring his old teacher that "the capital of friendship that we have accrued over the decades" would not depreciate, and inviting him to Switzerland: "Once you are here, those around you will make every effort to ensure that you don't feel the heavy losses you have suffered as acutely, but rather can lead an orderly life here. You know how happy I am to share everything with you, all the more so since I feel a duty both to you and our science."

On March 4, 1939, Willstätter was permitted to leave Hitler's Germany, "like a plucked chicken"; his fortune remained behind. But rather than "share everything" with him, Stoll locked him into a contract that Willstätter, impoverished and, what was more, in Stoll's debt, could hardly turn down: "We make polite reference to the discussions held the previous week between yourself and the first of the signatories below and take the liberty of summarizing the results as follows," as a letter from Sandoz put it. "You have stated your willingness to grant our company an option on all your future inventions in the chemistry field, in other words to offer exploitation rights to these inventions to our company first." Everything that Willstätter thought up from that point forward was to potentially become the intellectual property of the Basel concern. This was the price that Stoll exacted for arranging asylum in Switzerland: "Thus we will have exclusive exploitation rights. In particular we will have the right to apply for a patent on the method or, if a patent already exists, to have it transferred to us." In return, Willstätter was entitled to a 3 percent share in the sales of products he developed, should these become eligible for a patent. Further, he received a base salary of a thousand francs per month. This was in return for his expertise, which he was obligated to offer up on demand in relation to all products in development at Sandoz.

But Willstätter, whom the writer Hermann Hesse described as being of "upright and courageous character," as "a great man and one of the very few who, before Hitler, had provided German professors and privy councilors with an example and a model," never again returned to his former level of productivity. He was a broken man, his life's work destroyed. He wasn't able to endure Basel and instead settled in Tessin, several hundred kilometers away, where he wrote his autobiography. Willstätter maintained contact with his former student, whose accomplishments, or at least his financial gains, had long since outstripped his own. The Jewish German chemist was all too dependent on Stoll's goodwill. "I know of course that in order to maintain the friendship my father put up with some things which in and of themselves he didn't think were right," wrote Willstätter's daughter, commenting on the broken relationship with Stoll in an embittered letter. On August 3, 1942, Richard Willstätter died of a heart attack.*

---

* For a long time not even the mortal remains of the Jewish-German Nobel laureate would find a final resting place. For years his ashes were kept in a box in a cabinet in Tessin by his impoverished housekeeper. In 1949 the brilliant man's eagerly awaited autobiography appeared, *Aus meinem Leben* (From My Life). It was edited by none other than Arthur Stoll, who in his afterword praised his own role in Willstätter's life and evoked their deep friendship. There is no mention of his buying-up of artworks—or of Willstätter's early ejection from the Sandoz supervisory board in Nuremberg in 1933.

10

THE OTHER RICHARD

WHILE WILLSTÄTTER LOST EVERYTHING, HIS STAR PUPIL Richard Kuhn saw the opposite happen: He went on to have a story-book career in the National Socialist system, which lent its support to "Aryan" scientists. In 1937, at just thirty-seven years old, Kuhn became director of the Kaiser-Wilhelm Institute for Medical Research (which after the war would become part of the Max Planck Society) and accepted a professorship in biochemistry at the University of Heidelberg. That same year he was awarded the Nobel Prize in Chemistry, but refused it with a cutting letter:

It was with the utmost displeasure that I received notice that the Royal Swedish Academy of Sciences had awarded me the Nobel Prize in Chemistry. The Academy cannot be unaware of the fact that by virtue of a decree issued by the Führer and Reich Chancellor on January 30, 1937, every German has been barred from accepting a Nobel Prize from now on into perpetuity. Under these circumstances I cannot view in the decision to award the prize the intention to honor a German scholar, but rather only an attempt to induce a German to defy his Führer's decree and thus commit a breach of faith. I must repudiate such an affront in the most forceful terms and hereby refuse to accept the prize.

At the bottom of the letter, Willstätter's protégé added, by hand, the turgid National Socialist slogan: "The Führer's will is our faith."

Kuhn's Nazi orientation showed itself again and again. Speaking before the Chemistry Society of Berlin in 1942, he ended his lecture with the words "We hold in our thoughts the men in whose hands our collective future lies: to the Duce, the Tenno, and our Führer, a threefold Sieg Heil." Kuhn took part in research into nerve and poison gases for Hitler's plans of global conquest and developed the chemical weapon Soman, the deadliest in the world.

For Stoll none of this was reason enough to break off contact with him. Did the Sandoz director inform his close confidant, who was deeply involved in ergot research, of the discovery of LSD as well? If so, it would have been of urgent interest to the Nazi scientist. Nineteen forty-three, the year in which the ultra-potent substance first saw the light of day, was a precarious point in time for the fascist regime in the heart of Europe. Hitler's extermination policy had brought the "Third Reich" to the edge of the abyss: Germany's cities lay in ruins, and the Wehrmacht had suffered a decisive defeat in Stalingrad. As a result, research into new unconventional weapons that would turn the tide of the war was running at top speed. This explicitly included the use of substances that had a strong effect on the human mind—and here there was a connection with Hitler himself. The dictator couldn't admit to making mistakes; whenever things went wrong, he always suspected betrayal. He sensed conspiracies everywhere. Attempts on his life, like the one made by Georg Elser, acting alone, in the Munich beer hall, reinforced this paranoid stance. "I'd like to know who this Elser guy is, what sort of person we're dealing with," Hitler had demanded of Reinhard Müller, head of the Gestapo. "Use all available means to get this criminal to talk. Have him hypnotized, give him drugs; make use of everything that our modern science has tried in this area. I want to know who the instigators are, I want to know who's behind this."

A confession needed to be coaxed out of Elser, and specifically a confession stating that he had concocted his assassination plan together with the British Secret Service—which in fact was not true. He was given the stimulant methamphetamine, which was supposed to loosen his tongue, but to no avail: Even though three medical specialists spent a full day and night "working on" the would-be assassin, over the course of which time they "injected substantial quantities of Pervitin . . . [h]is statement was always the same."

This wasn't the first time that the National Socialist regime had attempted to deploy a supposed "truth drug." As early as the Reichstag fire trial in 1933, the defendant Marius van der Lubbe had been given scopolamine, the alkaloid found in certain nightshades, which rendered the defendant submissive. Ever since then, researchers had been on the hunt for a substance that would tease secrets out of a person, even against his will—a substance that put the ego out of action so that the interrogation subject turned into a plaything of the interrogator.

In 1942 the search intensified: On July 27, at Britain's Government Code and Cypher School at Bletchley Park, a Victorian estate northwest of London, a German radio transmission from occupied Ukraine encrypted with the Enigma cipher machine was decoded: "Experiments to date of injecting [Soviet] paratroopers with scopolamine were successful," it stated. "Therefore attempts should be undertaken with mescaline, since these injections strengthen the effect by inducing intoxication.* This is a request from the SS commander in Ukraine to be supplied with mind-altering drugs by way of the SS pharmacist in the Reich Main Security Office."

---

* Mescaline is an alkaloid found in the Mexican peyote cactus that acts on the central nervous system, can trigger hallucinations, and has been used ritually and for medicinal purposes by the indigenous cultures of America for centuries. Dating back to the 1920s, Kurt Beringer at the University of Heidelberg experimented with it on volunteers. It was Beringer who first mentioned the idea of using mescaline as a truth drug: "The patient [has] the inclination . . . to blurt out things otherwise kept hidden and secret, to express himself in uninhibited manner, occasionally to make unasked-for confessions, as well as to admit freely to likes and dislikes" (Beringer, *Der Meskalinrausch*).

KAISER WILHELM·INSTITUT
FÜR MEDIZINISCHE FORSCHUNG
INSTITUT FÜR CHEMIE

HEIDELBERG   2o.11.43
TELEFON 4752

DIREKTOR PROF. DR. R. KUHN

Herrn Prof. Dr. A. Stoll
Chemische Fabrik Sandoz A.G.
Basel

Sehr geehrter Herr Professor Stoll !
        Für die Überlassung der 5 x 0,1 g
Ergotamintartrat, die wohlbehalten in meinen
Besitz gelangten, sage ich Jhnen meinen
besten Dank.
        Bei dieser Gelegenheit möchte ich
Jhnen noch mitteilen, dass wir am 8. Oktober
eine Tochter namens Linde bekommen haben.
Meine Frau und auch die Kleine befinden sich
wohl.
        Mit den besten Grüssen
                Jhr sehr ergebener
                Richardkuhn

Hitler's top biochemist receives ergotamine from Sandoz.

Did the Nazis try to make use of LSD, too? On November 20, 1943, Kuhn, who was substantially involved in the development of biochemical weapons for Hitler, wrote a letter to Stoll. In it he proudly announced the birth of his daughter, but the main purpose of the letter was something else: "My sincerest thanks for the shipment of the 5 x 0.1 grams of ergotamine tartrate, which I received safely."

Ergotamine was the substance Hofmann had used to synthesize LSD: 0.5 grams could be broken down to yield 250 milligrams of lysergic acid, and from there it was just a simple step to combine this with diethylamide. That would make 250 milligrams of LSD, or 250,000 micrograms—about 2,500 strong doses.

11

BRAINWASHING

IN THE EARLY FORTIES, AT THE AUSCHWITZ EXTERMINATION camp, Dr. Bruno Weber, head of the "Hygienic-Bacteriological Investigation Office" of the Waffen-SS, began conducting human experiments involving barbiturates, morphine products, and sulphonamides.* The impetus was the Gestapo's frustrating experience with their interrogations of Polish resistance fighters, who even under torture refused to talk. But Weber didn't find the longed-for truth drug, and another series of experiments was planned, this time at the Dachau concentration camp: "Chemical Methods for the Neutralization of the Will." Leading the charge was Dr. Kurt Plötner, a thirty-seven-year-old SS *Hauptsturmführer* and employee of the SS Ahnenerbe's Institute of Applied Research in Military Sciences (Institut für wehrwissenschaftliche Zweckforschung), a University of Leipzig–educated physician who had numerous publications to his name and was due to be made a professor. He received his new assignment from Himmler himself:

> Besides other means, Messkalin [*sic*] (synthetically produced) was used ... Messkalin had to be given unobtrusively so that the person being examined did not know that he was no longer master

---

* Barbiturates produce a dulling, anxiety- and tension-easing, sometimes soporific effect. Sulphonamides are synthetic antibiotics.

of his free will . . . P.E.'s [persons examined] got the Messkalin in smallest quantities mixed with liquor or coffee. Then a harmless conversation took place in the course of which they began to react in a different way after half an hour to one hour . . . The examining person succeeded in every case in drawing even the most intimate secrets from the P.E. when the questions were cleverly put.

Was one of these "other means" LSD, making its way from Stoll to the concentration camp by way of Kuhn? The search for the truth drug shifted into high gear when on July 20, 1944, another attempt was made on Hitler's life, the bomb that Wehrmacht officer Claus Schenk Graf von Stauffenberg detonated at the Führer's headquarters, the Wolfsschanze. The dictator survived, the coup attempt failed, and the Gestapo arrested hundreds of people. The key question for the Nazi regime in this last phase of the war was this: Who within its own ranks was friend, who was foe? Hitler was obsessed with the idea that in order to achieve the "Final Victory" promised by his propaganda, all he needed was to find out who was on the side of National Socialism and who was secretly working against it. If all those in opposition were sorted out, he claimed, then the war could still be won. But when questioning suspected officers, the Gestapo ran up against the limits of its capabilities. Even the use of old-fashioned torture, so-called *Verschärftes Verhör*—third-degree interrogation—offered no guarantee of coaxing everything out of them. The most brutal methods frequently led only to lies told out of necessity. But Plötner's series of experiments in Dachau didn't produce results fast enough. Before he could complete his experiments, American troops liberated the Dachau concentration camp in late April 1945 and his documents disappeared. For the moment.

PART II

WEAPON

12

THE TRIP CHAMBER

MORE THAN FIFTY MILLION PEOPLE LOST THEIR LIVES OVER the course of the Second World War. Hundreds of millions were wounded, in body and in soul. Just about everyone living on the European continent was forced to give up the life they had before; the social fabric was torn to shreds. How was this battered portion of humanity ever supposed to get back on its feet again? How could the wounds be healed, the millions of individual traumas worked through? How were people supposed to trust again, themselves and others? How would they build a new future together?

And wasn't there a fortune to be made, thought Arthur Stoll at his corporate headquarters in Basel, so long as one had the right product to offer? Was it possible that LSD could fit the bill? Sandoz started doing its own internal tests. First, volunteers were sought and a kind of trip chamber was set up, a "quiet room with window shades [and] places to sit and lie down." Adventurous chemists and staff members from the technical and sales divisions at Sandoz were invited into this room, where they were given LSD in low doses of between twenty and thirty micrograms. The subjects told a secretary about their sensations and inner experiences, and she typed it all up on her typewriter.

"Our task was to investigate the unique mental effect of LSD with psychiatric methodology, to clinically characterize it," Stoll wrote, describing the approach, and thanked his colleagues for "their

daring in the face of a little-known substance." Writing samples
were delivered, taste tests performed, reflexes tested, blood pressure
taken. How did it feel to lie down while on LSD? To stand up? To
walk around? An initial general picture emerged: After taking the
drug, a feeling of "calm, contemplative cheerfulness" set in. "If only
it were always like this," one volunteer was reported to say. LSD was
felt to be a "*Ferienfrühstück*!"—a "breakfast on holiday!"—that led to
a "pleasant carefree sensation." The reports of subjects' experiences
noted several instances of a "compulsion to laugh": "I just can't
control myself . . . my mouth, it just keeps twisting up [into a smile]
. . . For no reason I have to laugh. The impulse to laugh gets stronger,
it makes my body shake until tears come to my eyes." One lab assistant
recounted: "Existence was like a dream, as beautiful and pure as you
could ask for." For many it was enough "just to sit there." Another
volunteer reported, "[I] sensed moments when I lost myself in nature,
[watching] the flight of birds for example, with great childlike joy."
Even the aftereffects experienced after the initial sensation wore off
were positive: "Familiar things at home were freshly laid claim to with
delight, as if they were gifts. Music was experienced more intensely
than usual." Or simply: "I feel young and pretty and fresh."

Since only good experiences were recorded, there were no
physical side effects like elevated blood pressure, pulse rate, or
body temperature, and no dependence was formed, Stoll could
start nourishing hopes of a blockbuster therapeutic drug: LSD,
which "in unimaginably small doses influences the workings of
the emotions in a consistent manner," promised exactly what the
beaten-down population all over the world needed. Indeed, the
mysterious molecule offered "an abundance of unique alterations
to mental life."

The next stage of testing was to be conducted confidentially:
Sandoz couldn't let the competition find out about the potential
smash hit. "More than anything the enormous effectiveness justifies further trials." Arthur Stoll's son Werner worked as a doctor at
the cantonal sanatorium in Zurich, the Burghölzli, a facility once

referred to as an "insane asylum" that today is part of the Zurich University Psychiatric Clinic. His task now consisted of determining if the substance was just as effective for the mentally ill as it was for the healthy employees of "the factory." "Carefully selected individual patients" at his son's sanatorium received the medicine, sent over as "20 vials L.S.D. incl. 2 pipettes." Unlike at Sandoz, the subjects were not informed of what was happening to them: "The experiment is disguised as a new shock treatment," wrote Werner Stoll. The undertaking was so secret that even "colleagues [were] not told of it for the time being."

The results from these tests also left the drug developers feeling optimistic. A depressive, "constantly irritable and quick-tempered young maid," who was afflicted with "apocalyptic feelings, paranoid ideas," could be released, cured, after "three LSD trials." Same with a farmer diagnosed as "late-onset paranoid." A total of six patients received the novel medication in varying amounts, from a microdose of 10 micrograms to a strong dose of 130 micrograms.

His son's work fueled Arthur Stoll's expectations of a revolutionary psychotherapeutic drug. His belief that he had his hands on a game changer, a medicine the likes of which were seldom ever seen, grew stronger. Pressing down on him now was "a massive amount of questions that . . . pointed deep into the 'big' psychiatry of severe endogenous emotional disorders." Effectiveness against impaired brain function in old age was also to be tested. Arthur Stoll's manufacturer's intuition told him that Sandoz was in the early stages of developing one of the most promising medicines in the history of humankind. Many mental illnesses, psychoses, neuroses, and forms of depression seemed treatable with the ergot derivative.

But Sandoz's director had made a crucial mistake.

13

ALSOS

IN THE SPRING OF 1945 THE UNITED STATES FOUND ITSELF in an unexpected role. Hitler's Germany had fallen, the British Empire had been weakened by the war, and the United States stepped forward as the only power that could offer any opposition to the expansionist will of the other major victor of World War II, the Soviet Union. The Americans, who up until recently had been isolated on their own continent, were reluctant at first to take on this responsibility. Arthur Giuliani, who had to work so hard to find his bearings in bombed-out Berlin and was compelled to call on the help of former Nazis to get the drug situation in war-ravaged Germany under control, wasn't alone; many of his countrymen were in similar straits.

What the Americans lacked above all was information. What sort of strange, blasted Reich was this, anyway? What had they just walked into? What dangers did it hold—and what treasures? The Americans lacked even an effective centralized spy agency to supply them with such intelligence, and knew precious little about what went on outside their own borders. As a result the new arrivals had to pick things up as they went along and acquire tools on the fly that would enable them to justify their sudden position of preeminence as a new superpower. When it came to modern weaponry and soldiers, or economic might, no one could hold a candle to the United States, not even the dreaded Stalin. What was missing was know-how, and here the US looked at Germany with equal parts interest and concern. The country might have been in ruins, but for years on end the most capable scientists had pursued their work there. What sort of research had been carried out in Nazi Germany? Could the Americans use the results to survive in the nascent global conflict with the Soviet Union? The leadership of the US Marine Corps put the objective in the following terms: In occupying the defeated and demoralized country, their goal was "to exploit German science and technology for the benefit" of America.

One topic was of paramount interest: the development of the atom bomb. In order to win the race for the bomb themselves, the Americans had launched the top-secret Manhattan Project, which at one time had more than 130,000 people working on it. But at the start of 1945 it had still not succeeded in producing a functional nuclear weapon. Just how far had they come, the Nazi scientists who had been working feverishly on the development of new weapons for the "Final Victory"? The uranium atom had been split for the first time in Berlin in 1938, and the German physicists Werner Heisenberg, Otto Hahn, and Carl Friedrich von Weizsäcker were considered the leading men in their field. Time and time again Hitler had threatened to deploy wonder-weapons, which led the Americans to assume that the Nazis were a step ahead of them in the area of nuclear technology.

In order to obtain this superior knowledge for themselves, a secret mission was launched after the US invasion of Italy in September 1943 that was meant to investigate the Nazi successes in the area of atomic weapon research first and foremost, but also in the development of biological and chemical weapons. Under the code name Alsos, Greek for "grove," a team of intelligence officers consistently turned up wherever Allied troops had forced back the Wehrmacht. Their task was to track down leading scientists, detain them, and question them about their work; they were also to locate facilities for the production of fissile uranium or heavy water and confiscate materials and documents.

On February 24, 1945, the Alsos officers set foot on German soil for the first time. By then their mission had become a race against time. They had to take the leading Nazi scientists into custody before the Russians, who had already gained the German border in the East. On April 3, Alsos operatives reached Heidelberg, where they established a regional headquarters in the villa of a former Nazi functionary on Philosophenweg. The city had been spared by the war, and the American conquerors loved it, since it so wonderfully lined up with their notions of a fairy-tale Germany: Situated on the picturesque Neckar River, it had a castle, a centuries-old university, and vineyards covering the surrounding hills. A centrally located place of refuge, where one could both sense a lost grandeur and envision a new beginning.

"Heidelberg became an ideal vantage point from which to make forays in pursuit of our targets," wrote thirty-seven-year-old Carlo Henze, a captain in the US Medical Corps. "It allowed for thrusts north, east, and south as more and more German territory fell under American and British sway." Henze took part in the Alsos mission as an expert on biochemical weapons. In America he had interrogated captured Luftwaffe pilots and learned of the massive use of methamphetamine to enable longer flights and better concentration while dropping bombs. Since then he had been convinced that drugs would help decide the outcome of a war. He had also visited the top-secret military research facility at Camp Detrick, where the United States produced chemical weapons.

"In retrospect," he wrote in his recollections of that time, "one may have second thoughts about the morality of BW [biological weapons] research but such matters must be regarded in the context of their time. The Nazi war machine was deemed capable of anything if squeezed into a corner. Under such circumstances no defense establishment could afford to be unprepared." He added, "Presumably considerable spin-off came of it toward our knowledge of the spread of infectious diseases, vaccines, etc."

Henze's task in defeated Germany turned out to be difficult: "Unlike our colleagues in the physical sciences whose main targets were well known or even world famous as a result of their antebellum involvement in nuclear fission, we had little information for guidance. Vague and sporadic references came to us of alleged BW activities, but such reports usually originated with individuals who had no scientific background . . . We decided to play it by ear—checking individuals and institutions which we believed would give us clues, and following leads that we ourselves would develop."

Richard Kuhn necessarily came under scrutiny as a leading scientist residing in Heidelberg and former member of the scientific advisory committee reporting to Karl Brandt, Hitler's general commissioner for sanitation and health. In April 1945 he was questioned by the Alsos team in Heidelberg for the first time. Carlo Henze was also in touch with him—and for a very particular reason. Years earlier Henze had in fact worked at Sandoz in Basel, in the clinical research division, and from 1939 to 1941 he had been the factory's medical director, working directly under Arthur Stoll.

For Kuhn, running into Henze was an opportunity. As a former Nazi scientist, he was facing a choice: cooperation with the victors and possible immunity from punishment, or the defendant's bench in Nuremberg, where preparations for the tribunal for Nazi war criminals were under way. The directive from the commander of US forces in Europe was to "arrest and hold all war criminals," albeit "with some exceptions." Persons who for "intelligence or other military reasons" were relevant to the Americans remained at liberty. Many of them, like Hitler's rocket builder Wernher von Braun, were even permitted to emigrate to America and finish out their careers there as part of the secret Operation Paperclip program. Would Kuhn be able to present himself as one of these reputable exceptions?

Henze also stood to profit from their meeting. Finally he had found an expert in his specialized field of biochemistry—and part of his brief included the search for the putative truth drug. In the Cold

War, which was developing into a conflict over ideas, over the acceptance of this or that ideology, a substance that worked on human consciousness was of potential military relevance. Could Kuhn tell him anything about this?

Henze's top-secret work in Heidelberg met with such great interest in the American government that President Truman presented the Alsos agent with the distinguished Legion of Merit, a medal that dates back to George Washington's time, for "exceptionally meritorious service as a medical intelligence officer engaged in the collection of information concerning German research programs of major concern to the Allied forces."

14

THE MISSING BOX

LEO ALEXANDER, A PROFESSOR OF NEUROPSYCHIATRY WITH a bald patch and thick glasses, was sitting in an American military plane en route to Munich in May 1945 when he saw the Dachau concentration camp for the first time. A dozen years earlier Alexander had left Germany because he was of Jewish descent; now he was returning as an advisor to the American chief prosecutor in Nuremberg, come to call criminal Nazi doctors to account at the Doctors' Trial.

Up to this point there had been only rumors—of defenseless subjects being infected with viruses and bacteria, submersed in ice-cold water to the point of freezing to death, or locked in deadly chambers inside of which the air pressure could be altered at will. Was it all true? Would Alexander find evidence that he could present before the court in Nuremberg? The US Army had given the scientist just six weeks: He had to present his results by the end of June 1945, as that was all the time that was left before the trial was slated to begin.

The pilot flew a circle around the liberated camp so that Alexander could get a good look at it, the double row of narrow barracks, the camp's main road running in between them; the administrative wing, jutting out at a right angle; and the giant, once so feared roll-call yard, where the Nazis had developed a method of torturing inmates by making them stand for hours on end. This open field was

full of people, former inmates who for lack of strength or alterna-
tives still remained at the camp and waved at the military plane in
the hopes that it was bringing something to eat.

In the first days of his research, on visits to Dachau and places
around Munich, the American found nothing he could use in court.
Former workers at the concentration camp denied that human experimentation had taken place there. They had experimented on
pigs, that was all. Alexander remained skeptical, and when he found
out that secret documents belonging to Heinrich Himmler, head of
the SS, had been found in a cave in Austria, he moved heaven and
earth to see them. After days spent studying the files, the investiga-
tor found what he was looking for. He hit upon a network of criminal SS doctors who had carried out whole series of appalling tests
in Dachau, Auschwitz, Mauthausen, Buchenwald, and other camps.
Finally he had facts in hand, and by July 10, 1945, he had put together a
228-page report—and that was just the start. "German science presents a grim spectacle," Alexander wrote to his wife. "It was drawn
into the maelstrom of depravity of which this country reeks—the
smell of the concentration camps, the smell of violent death, torture
and suffering." In a later letter he added, "It sometimes seems as if
the Nazis had taken special pains in making practically every nightmare come true."

Dr. Kurt Plötner's notes on the truth drug were also examined.
In the run-up to the Nuremberg trials, which were set to begin on
November 20, 1945, and would go on for just under a year, Alexander
filed them in a binder and put the binder in a box, which he stowed
away in the American chief prosecutor's storage room for safekeep-
ing. But when he returned a short time later to get the documents on
the "Chemical Methods for Neutralization of the Will" and review
them in preparation for the trial, Alexander discovered to his surprise
and frustration that they were missing. At that point he knew nothing of a mission with the code name Alsos, had no idea that its agents
had access to the locked storage room—and wanted the subject kept

secret, for this pharmacological weapon could only be deployed if the other side learned nothing of its existence.

The experiments with mescaline and "other means" were never mentioned in the courtroom, and Plötner could be described as "trustworthy" without anyone objecting. Thus Alexander achieved only partial success. Nevertheless, the American professor had reason to be satisfied with his work, because in his time in Germany he also accomplished something crucial: His most important legacy is having drafted what has come to be known as the Nuremberg Code, a set of ethical guidelines considered the standard around the world for medical or psychological experiments that involve human subjects.

To begin with, it states, "The voluntary consent of the human subject is absolutely essential. This means that the person involved should have legal capacity to give consent; should be so situated as to be able to exercise free power of choice, without the intervention of any element of force, fraud, deceit, duress, over-reaching, or other ulterior form of constraint or coercion; and should have sufficient knowledge and comprehension of the elements of the subject matter involved, as to enable him to make an understanding and enlightened decision."

15

ADVISOR KUHN

ON MAY 25, 1948, ARTHUR STOLL TRAVELED FROM BASEL TO Heidelberg to deliver a lecture before an audience of psychiatrists, neurologists, and biochemists that, per Richard Kuhn, who was also in attendance, "all would remember fondly for a long time to come." It wasn't just academics who sat there listening to the Sandoz director. There were also men in uniform in the room, nothing unusual in those days in the picturesque city: In 1947 the US Army had established its European headquarters on the Neckar, and kept itself steadily informed of the goings-on in town.

Dr. John Clay, high-ranking advisor in the Chemical Division at the European Command Center, reported on Stoll's lecture and on a "powerful hallucinatory agent" presented therein with which experiments had been conducted, the "results" of which "appear[ed] very promising"—this from a letter marked *TOP SECRET*. "The synthesized substance is called LysergSaure-Diathylamid [*sic*]. Its laboratory code is LSD-25," Clay wrote, and concluding the letter, promised to "closely monitor all future studies at Sandoz Laboratories that could be beneficial to psychological warfare themes." Regarding the source who had been of help to him in evaluating Stoll's remarks, Clay declared, "Our agent on the inside has well proven his agility and scientific worth without compromising his delicate position."

Richard Kuhn's work for the US military ramped up after that. In the summer of 1948, US forces even offered him a job. The terms were spelled out in a letter bearing the letterhead of the "Office of Military Government, 7780th OMGUS group, Stuttgart," with Kuhn's signature at the bottom: "I hereby accept the position of scientific advisor in the field of biochemistry for the military government, Land Wuerttemberg-Baden, at a salary of DM 972 per month."* Now the former Nazi scientist found himself under the official protection of the victorious power, and received, on top of his salary, other perks like travel permits for "transport of scientific material, scientific consultations."

Of all the tasks Kuhn was supposed to take on for the Americans, the main one was to keep an eye on Sandoz's future course of action. Dr. Clay wasn't pleased with the company's plan to bring LSD onto the market as a medicine and advertise it to the public. Nor was the US military happy when Stoll next gave a lecture in Switzerland before both the Swiss Society of Psychiatry and the Association of Physicians in Zurich with the title "The New Hallucinatory Agent." This could attract the attention of hostile nations, Clay suspected. It was to be feared that the Soviet Union might want to use the drug "for purposes other than [medical] treatment." Clay issued an urgent call: "We should act quickly to gain the needed amount of this drug

---

* Washed clean of his Nazi sins by the USA, Kuhn was not denied international honors in the future, and when in 1949 the Nobel Prize that he had refused in 1939 out of devotion to Hitler was again awarded to him, he gratefully accepted it. In the fifties Kuhn traveled to the US several times, was a guest professor at the University of Pennsylvania, advised the American armed forces on the development of their chemical weapons arsenal, and signed a consulting contract with an American company worth $15,000 per year. In 1950 Kuhn again became professor of biochemistry in the faculty of medicine in Heidelberg, as well as director of the Max Planck Society for Medical Research, the Federal Republic of Germany's successor organization to the Kaiser-Wilhelm Institute, which ended along with the National Socialist state.

as quickly as possible and to do whatever is necessary to keep it out of the hands of undesirables."

It wasn't hard for Kuhn to satisfy American expectations of him when it came to Sandoz. He was soon named to a post at the company, and on top of the salary he received from the US, he began pocketing an additional 1,500 Swiss francs a month for the "scientific collaboration begun between us and as an advance on the inventor's share due to accrue to you later on," as Arthur Stoll wrote from Basel. Kuhn didn't receive the salary directly; rather it was transferred, "as instructed by [him], to the postal check account in the name of [his] sister-in-law." Thus when it came to ergot research, Stoll and Kuhn were working even more closely together—a collaboration that would prove fatal to the development of LSD.

16

PORK CHOPS

THE CONFRONTATION BETWEEN EAST AND WEST GREW MORE tense. Without notice, overnight on June 24, 1948, the Russians switched off the high-tension power lines that ran between the Zschornewitz power plant in the Soviet-occupied zone and the Western sectors of divided Berlin. The power generators in West Berlin couldn't compensate for the missing electricity, and the lights went out from Wannsee to Kreuzberg. At six o'clock the following morning the Red Army blockaded all railroad tracks and roads leading into the Western sectors of the former capital of the Reich. Soviet patrol boats moved out onto the Havel to put a stop to traffic crossing the river as well.

The Western Allies weren't prepared for this escalation, though it's possible they could have seen it coming. The obstructionist policy that Arthur Giuliani—among others—had already experienced a year and a half earlier in disputes with his Russian colleagues was now being practiced on the greatest possible scale. Now people in the French, British, and American zones were stuck there without any supplies; no emergency plan existed, no one knew how the more than two million residents of West Berlin, fully dependent on shipments from outside the city, were supposed to be fed. On the RIAS radio station, the American commandant in charge of the city announced, "I don't yet know the answer to the current problem—not yet—but this much I do know: The American people will not allow the German people to starve."

If up until this point the Cold War had mainly been a threat hanging in the air, the Berlin Blockade was its first clear manifestation. The solidarity that at one time had existed between the US and the Soviet Union, who had worked together to defeat Hitler, was now gone. Germany was a battleground once more, this time in a war between Moscow and Washington. No one knew how far the other side would go. Colonel Donald Galloway, a high-ranking official in US intelligence, summed the situation up: "We have to get a picture of the Red Army's divisions as soon as possible, their arms, their fighting morale, their supply depots. They have to be made transparent in no time, as legible as an open book! To attain this goal all means are justified!" A secret commission assembled by President Truman described the precarious situation thusly: "It is now clear that we are facing an implacable enemy whose avowed objective is world domination by whatever means and at whatever cost. There are no rules in such a game. Hitherto acceptable norms of human conduct do not apply. If the United States is to survive, long-standing concepts of 'fair play' must be reconsidered. We must develop effective espionage and counterespionage services and must learn to subvert, sabotage and destroy our enemies by more clever, more sophisticated and more effective methods than those used against us."

Alarmed by this development, in June 1948 the fifty-one-year-old Brigadier General Charles E. Loucks, head of the US Army Chemical Center, made the trip across the Atlantic to Heidelberg in order to coordinate American chemical warfare using the city as his base. Kuhn became an important contact for him as well. The high-ranking military man wasn't interested in the German's past. "I was under the impression that Professor Kuhn had been cleared of his Nazi complicity." The general was however very much interested in LSD as a potential new kind of weapon against the Russians, for which reason Kuhn put him in contact with Sandoz. In order to remain under the radar, the general took an unusual step: "Went back to the house and put on civilian clothes," he confided to his diary. In the afternoon his wife, Pearl, took him to the Heidelberg train station, and at nine o'clock in the evening Loucks reached his hotel in Switzerland. There he lit a fire in the fireplace and met the next morning with Arthur Stoll's son Werner, who was happy to tell him all about LSD and even handed him a free sample. Loucks's conclusion after receiving a firsthand briefing was that LSD was a substance that could be of use in two ways: first as a means to gain advantages in interrogation situations, and second as a tool for so greatly bewildering an enemy combatant that it put him out of action without killing him—a potentially new form of warfare. Excited, Loucks headed back to Heidelberg and met Kuhn for a debriefing over lunch: "pork chops."

With the detonation of the first Soviet atom bomb in 1949, the situation escalated further: The nuclear arms race began. An atmosphere of mistrust and paranoia began to take hold, especially since the nuclear know-how seemed to have come from a breach of secrecy in the West. In a sensational trial in New York, the American couple Ethel and Julius Rosenberg were sentenced to death for committing espionage for the Soviet Union and were executed by electric chair. Also in 1949 the Chinese civil war ended in victory for the Communists and Mao proclaimed the People's Republic: a shock for the white establishment in America. Questions of security that no one could have imagined a short time before were fervently discussed: What if "someone planted an A-bomb in one of our cities and we had twelve hours to find out from a person where it was. What could we do to make him talk?"

A race had long since begun, one that Arthur Stoll had never wanted but that he himself had kicked off through his dealings with Kuhn: It was a race between researchers on the one hand, who were studying LSD as a medication for treating illnesses of the mind, and on the other hand agents of the American military, who wanted to deploy it as a pharmacological weapon in the Cold War.

17

LSD IN AMERICA

IN 1949 THE VIENNESE NEUROLOGIST OTTO KAUDERS PRE-
sented LSD at a conference at the Boston Psychopathic Hospital.
Kauders's sensational assertion was that the substance induced a
"model psychosis" that lasted several hours. With the drug's help,
illnesses of the mind could for a limited time period be "produced"
in healthy test subjects and studied. The Harvard professor Max
Rinkel, who had gained renown for his work on Pervitin, was so fascinated by what he heard that he contacted Sandoz right away and
placed a large order.

What happened next was the first trip taken on American soil,
experienced by Dr. Robert Hyde, a colleague of Rinkel's. More than
one hundred trials with test subjects followed, and in May 1950
Rinkel gave a report on his results at the annual gathering of the
American Psychiatric Association in Detroit. Confirming Kauders's
theory, Rinkel declared that LSD induced "a transitory psychotic dis-
turbance" that could be used for the study of mental problems. The
term *psychotomimetic* started making the rounds: a substance that
made it possible to look at the psyche as if under a magnifying glass.
What was more, this new approach to the use of LSD supported the
view that depression and schizophrenia might result from material
causes. Where before the brain had been considered an electrical
affair and treated with electroshocks, now the idea was catching on
that it wasn't physics calling the shots in our heads after all, but bio-

chemistry. The theory went like this: Similar to LSD, which had an effect at even the tiniest doses, there were substances that occurred naturally in the body, also in minuscule amounts, which played crucial roles in a person's mental well-being. This theory was confirmed with the discovery of neurotransmitters.* This seemed the great promise of LSD: With its help, scientists would find out more and more about the way the brain functioned.

At the same time, then, that the US military was setting its sights on the ergot derivative, it was unleashing euphoria in medical circles.

"Never before in the history of science," wrote the psychotherapist and consciousness researcher Stanislav Grof, "was a single substance so promising for so many disciplines." The ability to make invisible phenomena more tangible and subject them to scientific inquiry gave LSD unique potential as an instrument for diagnosis as well as a tool for exploring the human mind. "For neuropharmacologists and neurophysiologists this discovery signified the beginning of a golden age in which it would be possible to solve certain mysteries regarding . . . the tricky biochemical interactions of cerebral processes."

A research boom began. Where the Sandoz archives note a mere eleven publications on LSD from 1943 to 1950, in the following ten years there were more than a thousand. Albert Hofmann responded to the shift with enthusiasm and expressed the "happiness and gratification that any pharmaceutical chemist would feel on learning that a substance she or he had produced might possibly develop into a valuable medicine. For the creation of new medicines is the goal . . . ; therein lies the meaning of her or his work."

---

* For the first time the mechanism was discovered by which serotonin acts on the mussel. The messenger substance is responsible for opening the contracted mussel shell in relation to the ocean's current—it thus has a "relaxing" character. Following this discovery there was speculation as to whether serotonin also occurs in humans, and it was determined, surprisingly, that the neurotransmitter functions primarily in the brain, where, as the "happiness hormone," it likewise has a relaxing effect.

Sandoz's prospects for turning LSD into a successful product seemed excellent. Psychoses and cases of depression, epilepsy, and schizophrenia were constantly on the rise. More and more people in the late 1940s were ending up in psychiatric institutions and hospitals. All over the world physicians were searching feverishly for methods to influence neural processes in the brain and bring about changes in the mental state.* Psychiatry, prior to this point a discipline at the far end of the medical spectrum that was practiced in isolated places called "insane asylums," moved to the mainstream of society and attained ever-higher standing in universities as well. Psychiatric expertise was now in vogue; professional groups like the American Psychiatric Association gained influence. Rising prosperity and the spread of health insurance networks boosted the demand for medications. In the US, the most important market for pharmaceuticals, the number of people with insurance rose by a factor of ten between 1940 and 1960, from 12 million people to more than 120 million.

On the drug producers' end, rising investment, both public and private, led to a soaring rate of innovation. There was a constant stream of new discoveries; new products were coming onto the market all the time, including those that might compete with LSD. In 1950 the French company Rhône-Poulenc synthesized chlorpromazine, a ring of nitrogen and sulfur flanked by two benzene rings composed of organic hydrocarbon, a so-called plenothiazine that had come out of paint manufacturing. It blocks the dopamine receptors in the brain and produces a sedative effect—a new form of tranquilizer. Soon there was no stopping its triumph. Ever more frequently doctors began using the medicine sold under the brand name Thorazine to treat

---

* The first to raise the possibility of alleviating mental and emotional disturbances through the administration of medication was the German psychiatrist Emil Kraepelin in his 1883 study "Über die Einwirkung einiger medikamentöser Stoffe auf die Dauer einfacher psychischer Vorgänge" (On the Effect of Certain Medicinal Substances on the Duration of Simple Mental Processes); he favored opium.

psychoses and depression. The number of occupied beds in psychiatric hospitals, which up to that point had been rising continuously, sank by half. All of a sudden sadness was nothing more than a chemical imbalance in the head that could be straightened out pharmacologically. Anyone who had troubles could just swallow a sedative powder and the sorrow that originated in the receptors would dissolve, just like that.

Ever more psychopharmaceuticals were developed. These drugs didn't target the cause of mental disorders, as LSD promised to do, but were merely limited to providing periods of relief and producing pleasant feelings artificially. Drug stores and pharmacies were flooded with benzodiazepines: anxiety-easing sleeping pills and sedatives like, for example, Valium—"Mother's little helper." The downside of these drugs, in terms of their users' health, was that they put the mind in a fog and had to be taken regularly, often for the rest of the patient's lifetime, with severe side effects.

Stoll decided that it was high time to bring LSD out onto the market. The substance had been around for nine years, but was still just a trial medication, not available for purchase. Meanwhile other ergot products like Gynergen and hydergine were Sandoz bestsellers and made up 40.4 percent total sales. Thanks to ergot "the factory" had blossomed into a global corporation, with forty international subsidiaries. "And so today with regard to ergotamine we possess an almost exclusive monopoly," Arthur Stoll stated with satisfaction. Soon the sales generated by the pharmaceutical division would exceed those from paint manufacturing for the first time. For this success he was named president of the board of directors.

Thus motivated, the newly minted CEO traveled to the US in the spring of 1950, his bags packed with the strongest substance in the world. In Manhattan he stayed at the Plaza Hotel on Fifth Avenue, where he met with Carlo Henze, the former Alsos agent—and now head of the New York Sandoz subsidiary. In a room with a view of Central Park, the two discussed the pending approval of LSD by the Food and Drug Administration (FDA).

Stoll's first public appearance in America was at Harvard, where on May 9, 1950, he gave a lecture hosted by the Department of Chemistry, with the title "Recent Investigations on Ergot Alkaloids." In the audience sat the assembled professoriate of the elite university's science departments, though one attendee in particular was to play a crucial role in what was to come. This was the respected physician Henry K. Beecher, who held the world's first chair in anesthesiology. In World War II Beecher had served as a major in the US Army Medical Corps in Africa and then Europe and in February 1947 had risen to the role of advisor to the US War Department. In this capacity he was among those to receive from Washington the highly classified report on the Dachau drug experiments that was suppressed during the Nuremberg trials. For three years, from 1947 to 1950, the Harvard professor had been unable to complete the task given him by the War Department of determining which "other means" alluded to in the report had been administered by Dr. Plötner to "facilitate probing of the subconscious" and "make it possible to get at deliberately suppressed information." The US military ruled mescaline out: It couldn't be administered surreptitiously on account of "certain side actions"—like nausea and a bitter taste in the mouth—"which would make it possible for the properly informed security officer to detect himself that he might be in an abnormal state." But as Beecher sat there at Harvard listening to Stoll's remarks on a tasteless and odorless substance called LSD, a lightbulb went off. He immediately wrote his contact in the Defense Department (the newly established successor to the War Department): "I have not been forgetful of the study you mentioned to me . . . concerning an examination of agents that might be used in narcoanalysis or for use as 'truth sera.'"

In Washington this reply met with burning interest. By that point there were rumors circulating in the nation's capital that Russian agents were using drugs to make people compliant. Supposedly there were more than a hundred thousand scientists in the Soviet

Union at work on the development of methods for manipulating the human will and reprogramming the brain.*

On June 25, 1950, soon after the conclusion of Stoll's lecture tour, which had also taken him to Philadelphia, Cornell University, and the American Chemical Society in New Jersey, as well as to Chicago and Minneapolis, the Korean War began—and the fight for the brains of the people of the world escalated. North Korean forces attacked the South; within three days, Seoul, the South Korean capital, fell. Within a short amount of time nearly the entire peninsula had been overrun by Communist troops. When the United States intervened militarily on the side of the South while the Chinese supported North Korea, fear spread of a third world war. In Germany people began stock-piling sugar and flour. Sensational television footage reached the public: With cameras rolling, captured American pilots accused the US government of committing war crimes, specifically of de-ploying biological weapons. Speculation ran wild: What had the Chinese interrogation specialists done to the downed pilots to get them to make such statements? Were they secretly drugging them? An article in the *Miami News* popularized the term "brainwash-ing": The Communists now had techniques at their disposal "to put a man's mind into a fog so that he will mistake what is true for what is untrue, what is right for what is wrong . . . until he ulti-mately becomes a robot for the Communist manipulator."

America in these first few years of the 1950s was a nation col-lectively holding its breath, anxiously asking itself what would happen next. The mounting paranoia was stoked by Joseph McCarthy, a Republican senator, who claimed that the entire government was

---

* For example, in the Soviet-directed show trial against the Hungarian arch-bishop and dissident József Mindszenty in Budapest, devious means were supposed to have been used: Mindszenty, so the suspicions went, was not of sound mind, but rather under the influence of drugs when he pled guilty to some of the charges listed in the indictment for subversion, espionage, and currency offenses.

infiltrated by Communists. As alleged proof he cited a list he claimed to have in his possession with the names of 205 persons who were members of the Communist Party and worked in the US State Department, determining its policy. This claim turned out to be fake news, but it earned McCarthy enough media attention to continue his campaign. "We've been at war with Russia for some time now," he declared ominously and denounced the Socialist enemy, who was everywhere, undermining the order of society. He accused Democratic presidents Roosevelt and Truman of high treason and spread his conspiracy theory so adroitly that it became a determining factor in American domestic politics. In the House of Representatives, the House Committee on Un-American Activities combed through every aspect of American society, looking for Communist infiltration. Not even Hollywood was spared from its scrutiny. Stars like Charlie Chaplin and Orson Welles left the United States. The playwright Arthur Miller refused to name names of other writers who had taken part in Communist meetings and was convicted of contempt of Congress. Three years earlier, Miller had turned the experience of watching his colleagues being forced to testify before the committee into his play *The Crucible*, which premiered in 1953 and examined McCarthyism against the backdrop of the witch trials in seventeenth-century Salem, Massachusetts.

Back at Harvard, Henry K. Beecher was swept up by the spirit of the time and believed that the moment had come to carry out human experiments on American soil—and indeed with the very substance to which Stoll had introduced the audience at Harvard. In his study "Drug-Induced Mood Changes in Man," Beecher summed up his approach in the first paragraph, writing of the "necessary experimental animal, *man*." Though he determined that at Harvard Medical School there were too few "healthy young volunteers" to test the "synthetic agents," he got around this obstacle by using Massachusetts General Hospital, where he was department chair: "We have an almost ideal set-up here in Boston for study of this problem," he wrote to the US Defense Department. Ethical questions were ignored from the beginning, as a colleague recalled. There were no consent forms for the patients who received LSD to fill out: The test subjects "weren't informed about anything." It's not surprising that nearly half of Beecher's subjects also suffered harm as a result of the powerful effects that came upon them from out of nowhere, their reactions ranging from becoming "mildly hostile and paranoid" to experiencing "acute panic." With his methods, Beecher risked causing "serious trauma" and "placed his unwitting subjects at risk by giving them dangerous doses dictated by the demands of secret research—all in violation of the Nuremberg Code." The Harvard professor had ignored these guidelines from the start, deeming them impractical. The goal of his experiments was "the development and application of drugs which will aid in the establishment of psychological control." The human experiments, whose results, for reasons of privacy protection, are still under seal in Harvard's archive, were financed with a grant of $150,000 from the US Army's Medical Research and Development Board.

At Sandoz, work continued on getting the medicine approved. Dr. Ralph Paul Bircher, known as Rudi, director of clinical pharmacology at the company's American subsidiary, wrote Albert Hofmann in fall 1952 from his office downtown to express his confidence: "LSD will sooner or later be a matter of some importance in New York." He asked his colleague for an essay, "about four typed pages," to send to the trade journal *Medical Horizons* as a PR measure. In it Hofmann should describe how he had discovered LSD and what therapeutic uses he expected it to have. "I'm of course very glad that interest in LSD is growing," Hofmann wrote back, and offered some thoughts about a name for the product. "What do you think, just between us for now, about the name 'Metapsychin' for LSD, now that 'Psychergin' and 'Ergopsychin' are ruled out on account of trademark protection?"

The Swiss chemist was still optimistic.

18

BRAIN WARFARE

IN THE END, NO NAME WAS EVER CHOSEN. ONE CRUCIAL REAson for this was what happened on April 10, 1953. On this gray, rainy day, the CIA director, Allen Dulles, gave a speech to alumni of Princeton University, where Albert Einstein had taught. In it he made clear the goals of the Central Intelligence Agency, founded in 1947 and still quite little-known. "Remarks by the Honorable Allen Welch Dulles on the Horrors of Brain Warfare," as the program luridly put it. America's top spy would not end up disappointing his audience of former Princetonians:

"Our government has been driven by the international tension we call the 'cold war' to take positive steps to recognize psychological warfare and to play an active role in it," Dulles's lecture began. "I wonder, however, whether we clearly perceive the full magnitude of the problem, whether we realize how sinister the battle for men's minds has become in Soviet hands. We might call it, in its new form, 'brain warfare.' The target of this warfare is the minds of men both on a collective and on an individual basis. Its aim is to condition the mind so that it no longer reacts on a free will or rational basis but responds to impulses implanted from outside. A conditioning of the mind is the objective, so that one can no longer react out of free will or on a rational level, but only on the basis of impulses implanted from without." It was of vital importance for the United States to understand these "brain perversion techniques" the Soviets were using so that the US might be able to apply them themselves all the more effectively. The American public, Dulles said, was still unprepared for such an approach: "Some of these techniques are so subtle and so abhorrent to our way of life that we have recoiled from facing up to them." Dulles declared, "Behind the Iron Curtain a vast experiment is underway to change men's minds," an experiment that included "the perversion of the minds of selected individuals who are subjected to such treatment that they are deprived of the ability to state their own thoughts. Parrot-like the individuals so conditioned can merely repeat thoughts which have been implanted in their minds by suggestion from outside. In effect the brain under these circumstances becomes a phonograph playing a disc put on its spindle by an outside genius over which it has no control." According to Allen Dulles, this "brain warfare" was the greatest challenge that America had ever had to face—a conflict that, to hear him tell it, would mean either the survival or the annihilation of the United States.

On April 13, 1953, three days after his talk, the head of the CIA launched a program for the covert use of biological and chemical materials. Its code name was MK-Ultra. And LSD was to play an important role in it.

19

CEO AND CIA

TO LEAD MK-ULTRA, AN OUTSIDER WAS CHOSEN, A MAN OF whom even today only a handful of photographs exist and who made only a single public appearance in his lifetime.

Born with a clubfoot, Sidney Gottlieb had grown up in the Bronx in impoverished circumstances, the child of Orthodox Jewish immigrants from Hungary. For twelve years he walked with heavy metal braces on his legs and wore a bulky, custom-made shoe. He developed a stutter at the age of seven, and was "viciously harassed" on the streets of his poor neighborhood. But his willpower, his resolve not to let others keep him down, was his salvation. He overcame the speech impediment by taking courses in public speaking at City College in Manhattan, and his physical handicap didn't keep him from devoting himself to folk dancing: He could execute the most complicated steps and call out the instructions without his voice leaving him in the lurch.

In 1940 Gottlieb graduated magna cum laude from the University of Wisconsin with a degree in Agricultural Science, having specialized in botany, organic chemistry, and dairy farming. He went on to earn a doctorate in biochemistry and tried to enlist in the army during World War II, but was turned away: "I felt I had a duty to serve, yet I couldn't convince anyone that I would not be hampered in my performance." Instead he met a Montessori teacher, married her, and moved to the outskirts of the nation's capital in the hopes that being in Washington's orbit would enable him to finagle a job for himself in government. That he of all people was chosen to head up MK-Ultra came as a surprise even to Gottlieb himself—after all, he was cut from a different cloth than the Ivy League-educated WASPs who tended to occupy the leadership positions at the CIA. But for *this* job an outsider was ideal—someone whom nobody knew, who had no social connections; someone who would dedicate himself completely, full of devotion and gratitude for the opportunity to be a part of this exciting, privileged, vetted world whose secret-bearing initiates gained access to restricted areas, research data, and funds.

To begin with, the fledgling spy sought to gain a general picture of things and looked at which drugs affecting the human mind had been deployed in war up to that point. It wasn't long before he got his hands on the results of Henry K. Beecher's experiments. By then Beecher, along with several others, had authored a report, "Information from Europe Related to the Ego-Depressants," in which Gottlieb read, "We already have excellent evidence that a discreet man of the highest integrity can be made indiscreet and to lose his integrity, without his knowledge by the secret use of some of the drugs we are studying . . . The drugs in question have powers far beyond those of alcohol."

Beecher's remarks on LSD as a weapon fascinated Gottlieb. Because the amounts needed were minimal, owing to the potency of the drug, it would "not be a difficult trick to sink a small container of this agent near the main outlet of water storage reservoirs, and the container arranged to 'excrete' a steady flow of the material over a period of many hours or days." It was unthinkable, the intelligence agent speculated, what would happen if Russian agents managed to drive the citizens of New York, Los Angeles, or San Francisco insane. "There is still the possibility of contaminating, say, the water supply of a bomber base, or more easily still, that of a battleship," Beecher continued. "It takes little imagination to realize what the consequences might be if a battleship's crew were so affected . . . I earnestly hope that the United States will not get behind in this field for want of an organized plan of attack."

It was clear to Gottlieb after reading Beecher's studies that the distribution of LSD had to be regulated. The fact that a foreign company had the patent on the potential secret weapon, and a Swiss company at that, didn't sit well with him. The Swiss, always going on about neutrality, were not to be trusted. What if Sandoz sold the drug on the other side of the Iron Curtain? The first thing Gottlieb did was to send his agent Ray Treichler, a diminutive man in an oversize suit, around to Sandoz's office on Charlton Street in New York City. The CIA man's visit left an impression there. Soon afterward, on May 14, 1953, Carlo Henze wrote to Albert Hofmann, "Lately we've started getting slightly 'cold feet' on matters related to LSD, because the interest of authorized and unauthorized people in this substance is far beyond normal measure ... I think we'll wait a little longer until we have a clearer sense of what LSD's future development will look like."

When, not long after this, the US military attaché in Bern reported that the Soviet Union had received the staggering amount of fifty million doses—a false lead, as it later turned out—Gottlieb put two agents on a plane. Arthur Stoll was more than a little surprised when the visitors turned up at "the factory" with a briefcase containing 240,000 dollars in cash and informed him that they wanted to buy up the company's entire supply of LSD: ten kilograms, or ten billion micrograms, around one hundred million doses. Stoll clarified that since the discovery of LSD his company had produced only forty *grams*. He did however propose to his guests that Sandoz could increase production to one hundred grams per week and sell to the US government. Never, the Swiss CEO assured the CIA men, would the substance find its way into Communist hands; up to now only Americans had shown interest in it. Stoll offered to keep the US authorities apprised of any larger orders, especially if they came from Eastern Europe. In conclusion, the CEO offered to treat this arrangement with the CIA "in the very strictest confidence." Satisfied, the agents departed. Shortly thereafter, Henze in New York contacted the FDA to inform them that Sandoz was no longer seeking approval of LSD as a medication.

Gottlieb decided to personally familiarize himself with the substance: "It made no sense to use the drug on others without having first experienced it myself." He took his first hundred micrograms dissolved in water in New York and felt "very good, focused, centered. My thinking, my thought process, was clear yet different; there was a fluidity to it that was unusual . . . and a feeling of complete euphoria took hold of me for several hours." He understood now that people who consumed LSD *unknowingly* would necessarily be unnerved by the strong effects of the drug, not being able to explain the sudden mental changes they were going through. In order to test such an approach, he started dosing his colleagues with LSD. Some he informed ahead of time, others he didn't—and in each case he studied the different reactions.

A wild time began at CIA headquarters near the White House. Monitored experiments featured two colleagues at a time, who would analyze their experiences. But less structured tests were also known to happen. Someone in the open-plan office might turn his back on the wrong person and, unbeknownst to him, wind up with a few hundred micrograms in his morning coffee. "It was a game with . . . the mind, and sometimes embarrassing things happened. Case hardened spooks would break down crying or go all gooey about the 'brotherhood of man.'" One neurotic agent described his trip as follows: "I was shaky at first, but then I just experienced it and had a high. I felt that everything was working right. I was like a locomotive going at top efficiency. Sure there was stress, but not in a debilitating way. It was like the stress of an engine pulling the longest train it's ever pulled." When the agent went outside, he saw "all the colors of the rainbow growing out of cracks in the sidewalk. [I] had always disliked cracks as signs of imperfection, but suddenly the cracks became natural stress lines that measured the vibrations of the universe." He saw people's faces differently from the way he had before and no longer felt defects or abnormalities to be unsightly: "Hooked noses or crooked teeth would become beautiful for that person. Something had turned loose in me, and all I had done was shift my attitude. Reality hadn't changed, but I had. That was all the difference in the world between seeing something ugly and seeing truth and beauty." Out for a drink with colleagues that evening to come down from the trip, the CIA man had a knot in his throat and didn't fight the tears that came to his eyes. "I didn't want to leave it. I felt I would be going back to a place where I wouldn't be able to hold on to this kind of beauty. I felt very unhappy." Because of these emotions the report on his experience stated that LSD had depressed him, but that missed the mark: "They didn't understand why I felt so bad. They thought I had had a bad trip."

And bad trips did occur. Paranoid agents who worked in counter-espionage and fundamentally distrusted everything and everyone fled the office, went to ground in Washington, and stayed missing for hours, afterwards giving accounts of cars mutating into monsters, their headlights transformed into terrifying eyes, like in a "[bad] dream that never stops—with someone chasing you," and dark evil things hidden everywhere. In this environment, it paid to be vigilant. One CIA staffer was reported to have "brought his own bottle of wine to office parties and carried it with him at all times," knowing that to leave his drink unattended could invite dire consequences. For those working around Gottlieb, "unwitting doses became an occupational hazard."

20

THE CASE OF FRANK OLSON

FOR ONE MAN, THE HAZARD PROVED FATAL. BY THE TIME
Christmas arrived in 1953, Dr. Frank Olson was dead. He had died
four weeks earlier, a consequence of his unwitting ingestion of
LSD, given to him by Sidney Gottlieb. Olson knew Gottlieb well—
they'd had the same mentor as students at the University of Wisconsin
and had worked together before. As a bacteriologist and expert on
chemical and biological weapons, Olson had led the Special Operations Division (SOD) at Camp Detrick, Maryland, the military
facility that received two hundred thousand dollars a year from the
CIA to develop poisons for assassinations and covert biochemical
operations.

On November 18, 1953, a week and a half before Olson's death, he
and Gottlieb and a handful of colleagues gathered for a conference
in a log cabin surrounded by water on three sides on Deep Creek
Lake at the foot of the Appalachians. The top-secret meeting—those
in attendance had to remove their Camp Detrick entry permits from
their windshields before arrival—was meant to be a brainstorming
session, though Gottlieb charged this term with special meaning.
They were there to talk about toxic substances that the SOD was to
produce for the CIA. Among other points of discussion, the deadly
shellfish poison saxitoxin was compared with the equally fatal
botulinum toxin: When used in assassinations, the latter had the

advantage of not unleashing its effect for eight to twelve hours, thus giving an agent a better chance of getting away undetected.

The second evening after they had arrived, the poison makers gathered at the Deep Creek Lodge bar for a fateful cocktail. Gottlieb's deputy served orange liqueur. In addition to the Cointreau bottle from which he poured his boss a drink, he kept a vial of LSD hidden under his lapel. Olson got a taste of it as well. The goal of the clandestine operation within the clandestine gathering was to find out how people charged with keeping secrets reacted when given LSD without knowing it and asked targeted questions.

Olson reacted poorly. In the dark, remote log cabin, he experienced a bout of paranoia when something he couldn't explain, something incredibly intense, began to take hold of him. He yelled at Gottlieb, called the CIA agents names—"You guys are a bunch of thespians"— lost his nerve, said more than he should have. Allegedly he revealed that the number of anthrax bombs that the US Air Force had ordered from Camp Detrick for its Korean operations totaled one million and that the knowledge on which America's biological weapons program was based came from Unit 731 of the Japanese army defeated in World War II, whose scientists had received immunity from prosecution in exchange for their information. The same poisons, he said, that Japan had dropped on Manchuria had been used by the US in the Korean War.

In saying all this, Olson had become a security risk, and he knew it. When he got back home the next morning, he confided in his wife, saying he had made "a terrible mistake." In desperation he tried to quit his job at Camp Detrick the following Monday, saying that he was "all mixed up" and lacked the "competence" for his work. But his superior refused to accept his resignation. Olson's intention had been to get himself out of the line of fire, but his behavior only served to put a bigger target on his back. Now he was caught in a downward spiral. Gottlieb was informed of Olson's rattled mental state and arranged for him to be taken to New York, where he was supposed to receive psychiatric care from a doctor close to the CIA.

But Dr. Harold Alexander Abramson's treatment, which consisted of doling out the barbiturate Nembutal—a strong sedative—and a bottle of bourbon, didn't bear fruit: Olson sank deeper into depression. He was convinced that the CIA wanted him dead because he knew too much and hadn't been able to stand the pressure.

What happened on the night of November 27–28, 1953, in room 1018A of the Statler Hotel in Manhattan, which Olson shared with Gottlieb's deputy Robert Lashbrook (the same man who had served him the LSD-laced Cointreau), remains unclear. To this day, researchers, prosecutors, journalists, and artists have tried, without success, to cast light on the mysterious circumstances of his death.

The facts are as follows: While Lashbrook was present in the same hotel room, the forty-three-year-old Olson, at around two-thirty in the morning, broke through the glass of the closed (!) window, fell ten stories, and landed on the sidewalk on Seventh Avenue, across from Penn Station. The bacteriologist lay on his back, one arm extended, fingers splayed, his legs close together and twisted to one side. He wore nothing but a white undershirt and white underwear, and blood issued from his mouth, nose, ears, even his pale green eyes. Olson tried to speak, but bubbles of blood were all that came out. The Statler's night manager knelt down next to him, and the dying man grabbed his arm and raised his head with an effort while his lips moved. "He wanted to tell me something," the night manager was later quoted as saying. "I leaned down closer to listen, but he took a deep breath and died."

Gottlieb's involvement in the death of his colleague could never be proven. Twenty years later, however, the spy agency did admit to having used LSD to manipulate people. President Gerald Ford invited Olson's widow and their children to the White House, apologized, and offered 750,000 dollars in compensation—payable if they agreed not to bring the matter of Frank Olson's final days before a court. The family took the deal.

21

MENTICIDE

SIDNEY GOTTLIEB DIDN'T LET SUCH INCIDENTS AS THE death of a colleague distract him. He now decided to widen the scope of his study of LSD to the greatest possible extent. This much was clear to him: lysergic acid diethylamide was not a truth serum of the kind the Nazis had dreamed of. Nor was it going to fulfill his boss Allen Dulles's wish for something "to change a mind radically so that its owner becomes a living puppet—a human robot—without the atrocity being visible from the outside." LSD defied such crude objectives, was harder to get a handle on. To use it to grill some-one for information, turn them, take complete control of them and compel them to commit the foulest of deeds without them remem-bering a thing afterward—the old intelligence officers' dream—just wouldn't work. The possibility that LSD could nevertheless be uti-lized as a weapon in interrogations, could unnerve people and get them to "do something ten percent more often than they would otherwise," seemed to Gottlieb quite promising—and he launched a comprehensive research program.

And so, starting in 1954, more than 150 universities and research institutions in the United States, Canada, Great Britain, and other countries began to look at LSD from every angle. Participants in this research included Georgetown University and George Washington University; the Universities of Maryland, Pennsylvania, Minnesota, Denver, Illinois, Oklahoma, Rochester, and Texas; Harvard, UC

Berkeley, Stanford, Columbia, New York University, MIT, Cornell, Florida State, and Johns Hopkins; and many more. The key covert feature of the extensive project was that the scientists didn't know who they were working for. Without their realizing it, their results all landed on Gottlieb's desk. To pull this off, the CIA man used a trick: He had front organizations set up that financed the cost-intensive studies and were sent the results—but their connection to him remained hidden. This method had grave consequences. A study that was secretly backed by MK-Ultra was no longer an un-biased study, even if the scientists carrying it out never heard the name of their patron.

Gottlieb called his individual research initiatives "subprojects." There were at least 149 of them over the years, and they dealt with topics as various as the altering of behavioral patterns, influencing memory capacity, the promotion or inhibition of "anomalous" be-havior, altering personality structure or sexual preferences, assessing susceptibility to influence or level of discomfiture, or producing dependencies. They looked at techniques for undermining a person's self-worth and getting them to betray their principles; they studied the effects of radical isolation on intellectual functioning.

Conferences were held at which scientists discussed their find-ings, not knowing whose hands they were playing into. It was the most systematic research that had ever been conducted in the field of human consciousness. The intelligence agency's misuse of the Emmental-grown ergot derivative functioned like a key to a field of knowledge in which the Americans were soon unsurpassed. Ever more precise and effective protocols and guidelines were developed concerning the suppression of individuals. The head of MK-Ultra managed to turn the previously green agents of US intelligence into highly trained experts who carried themselves with an air of sophis-tication and employed advanced manipulation techniques. Thanks to Gottlieb's manic activity, the CIA developed into a one-of-a-kind research institution; its agents learned about the people they were tasked with controlling, acquiring a superiority in knowledge that no one could match. America took a very close look at *Homo sapiens* through Gottlieb's LSD magnifying glass, and the "mind control gap" between the US and the Soviet Union, which before had been regarded as superior in this area, was more than closed. "I outlined to you the possibilities of augmenting the usual interrogation methods by the use of drugs, hypnosis, shock, etc., and emphasized the defensive aspects as well as the offensive opportunities in this field of applied medical science," as the CIA director, Dulles, described these activities. If knowledge is power, then the CIA, by gathering more intelligence on how to influence the human mind than any other organization, truly did develop into an intelligence agency.

In the name of freedom, the CIA would in the future interfere everywhere Communism threatened to take hold. So began an era of coups d'état, covert interference, and even elimination of key figures deemed disagreeable. Proof exists of the use of high doses of LSD outside US borders on a total of thirty-three individuals in six different operations, intended to unnerve the person targeted to such an extent that they were incapacitated, divulged information, or did damage to their own reputation as a result of their strange behavior. One such instance involved a troublesome professor in South America who received an unannounced visit at his office at the university from a woman who pricked him on the wrist with a needle and left immediately thereafter. An ambulance was already waiting outside the front entrance to the building, but the professor's students managed to sneak him out the back entrance and take him home, where his psychotic episode lasted for a week. Even though he eventually returned to his post, it took him several years to regain the credibility that he had lost that day as a result of his erratic behavior: breaking glasses, pouring water on colleagues, speaking unintelligibly.

Even after the fact the scientists who received financing through Gottlieb's foundations did not learn that they had served as his stooges and that their experiments, as apolitical as they might have seemed to them, possibly found uses that they wouldn't have dreamed of. The psychiatrist Adam Hoffer, who conducted ground-breaking studies with LSD and its use in the treatment of alcoholism at a hospital in the remote town of Weyburn in the then socialist-run Canadian province of Saskatchewan, later said naïvely, "Why would they want to come to a hick place like Saskatchewan to look for what we might be doing? I have the idea that they didn't even know we existed." But Gottlieb probably knew quite well what was happening in the wilds of Canada three thousand kilometers from Washington, because by way of the Rockefeller Foundation—one of Gottlieb's conduits—he was financing Hoffer's studies with a generous $300,000.

It made no difference to Gottlieb whether or not experiments were conducted in an ethically unobjectionable manner, as they were in Saskatchewan. He was interested in the result, in learning whether the knowledge gained would further his understanding of how LSD could be deployed in the service of United States national security. Thus he also paid for tests like those at McGill University in Montreal, where Dr. Ewan Cameron, later president of the World Psychiatric Association, tried out bizarre methods for the treatment of schizophrenia. A total of fifty-three patients were put into a monthlong (!) coma, then subjected to so-called de-patterning: powerful electroshock treatments combined with high doses of LSD. Once the brain had been "wiped clean" in this way, Cameron began the process of reconditioning, which he called "psychic driving." Again he sedated his patients and locked them in a "sleep room," where he played a tape of recorded messages on speakers placed underneath the patient's pillow, at first negative:

[Name of test subject], you don't get along with people. You have never gotten along with your mother; she made you do what she wanted and you could never win out against her. You have always felt inadequate, and have been jealous of other people who felt that they had it better than you.

Spliced together to form an infinite tape loop, these psycho-messages were repeated until the patient showed resistance. After ten days at the earliest came the switch to a positively charged message:

[Name of test subject], you want to be free like other women . . . As you think about your relations with your mother, you see that you are now grown up, that your mother is no longer a threat to you, and you can be free to deal with her as a grown-up instead of trying, as in the past, to manipulate her as a child. [Name of test subject], you like to be with people, you like to be close to them, you like to reach out to them and touch them.

According to Cameron the rate of repetition for both the negative and positive messages ranged from "between 250,000 to 500,000 times during the course of the exposure." Cameron compared this approach, which calls to mind the nightmare scenarios in Stanley Kubrick's film *A Clockwork Orange*, with "the breakdown of the individual under continuous interrogation"—and in so doing made his research all the more interesting to the CIA.

Another institution that Gottlieb enlisted for his experiments was the Narcotic Farm, a facility in Lexington, Kentucky, established in 1935 and conceived of as a model institution for addicts. The imposing main building, a retro-futuristic redbrick spaceship plopped down on a thousand acres of lush bluegrass among hundreds of well-fed cows, was equipped with tennis and basketball courts, softball fields, a pottery studio, a bowling alley, pool tables, and a boxing ring—all open for the therapeutic use of the opiate-abusing hustlers and heroin-shooting street prostitutes of New York and the Dilaudid-addicted housewives and drugstore cowboys of the rural South.* In addition to the one thousand inmates there were five hundred voluntary visitors who checked themselves in for six months to fight their addiction. Narco, as the

---

* Dilaudid (hydromorphone) is a highly addictive semi-synthetic opioid.

facility was popularly known, was renowned outside its walls for its music rooms, in which jazz greats like Sonny Rollins and Chet Baker, there to take the cure, jammed and gave celebrated concerts for the locals, while the Beat writer William Burroughs sat over by the window, looked out at the silos, and tried to kick his heroin habit.

The idea behind Narco was rehabilitation, a progressive approach that had never existed in America before and that lined up with the nation's new understanding of itself as a place where science and ingenuity could fix anything, including addiction. This approach faced a problem, however, in the form of the draconian drug laws written by Harry J. Anslinger, which called for a minimum sentence of two years for a first-time conviction for drug possession, no matter what illegal substance the person convicted was caught with. Even if criticism of the FBN chief grew louder as years went by and he was later criticized for having "led [the US] to treat scientific questions, at least in the area of drugs, the way such matters were handled in the Middle Ages," the Narcotics Control Act of 1956, which he helped push through Congress, went so far as to set the minimum penalty for drug offenses at five years. As a consequence of this, Narco was soon bursting at the seams, and in place of time- and cost-intensive rehab offered little more than violent detention.

The core component of the facility was the Addiction Research Center (ARC), at the time it was established the only lab in the world dedicated to the comprehensive study of the phenomenon of addiction. Beneath the high, vaulted ceilings, the doctors delved into countless questions: How does tolerance form? What happens in the brain when addiction occurs? How does a person's behavior change while he's on various substances? Conferences were held and committees formed, like the "Committee on Drug Addiction and Narcotics" that convened in January 1955, which also included officials from Anslinger's FBN. The ARC was led by a close acquaintance of Gottlieb's, the pharmacologist Harris Isbell, who carried out numerous human experiments in the 1950s with millions of tax dollars funneled to him by the CIA. In line with the racist orientation of prohibition policy, Isbell preferred to use Black patients, even though they constituted a minority among Narco inmates. When, in the seventies, he was called to account for his activities, he conceded that "the ethical codes were not so highly developed" in those days. He largely dispensed with the declarations of consent that the Nuremberg Code requires. The groundbreaking studies that he carried out at Gottlieb's direction turned on questions of dosing and tolerance buildup. In order to obtain results that would satisfy the CIA, he put inmates on LSD for up to eleven weeks, seventy-seven days in all. To maintain the same degree of response, he had to up the dose, doubling, tripling, quadrupling the initial amount given. He also had his subjects try out unconventional substances that Gottlieb sent him, among them bufotenine, a hallucinogenic toxin found in toads. "I will write you a letter as soon as I can get the stuff into a man or two," he cynically wrote to the MK-Ultra chief. If the prisoners made it through the experiment, their "voluntary" participation paid off. Isbell bribed his patients, who were in his care in order to get off drugs, with precisely that: those addicts who volunteered for an experiment were rewarded afterward with the substance they asked for, in most cases heroin—and indeed, heroin of a quality that they would never find on the street. To get it, the human guinea pigs were allowed to knock on a little window in the hallway of the ARC, the so-called drug bank, where they were told how much heroin or morphine they had earned through their cooperation—or how much was still left in their "account." Then they were asked in what form they would like to receive their "withdrawal." "If you wanted it in the vein, you got it there," recalled the Black inmate Eddy Flowers, who had landed in Gottlieb and Isbell's clutches at age nineteen.

22

OPERATION MIDNIGHT CLIMAX

DECEMBER 17, 1953, WAS AN ICE-COLD DAY IN NEW YORK. AT three o'clock in the afternoon, the temperature was 25 degrees Fahrenheit, and Sidney Gottlieb was on his way to an apartment building in Greenwich Village carrying four thousand dollars in cash. Even in frigid weather this was a lively part of town. "The Village" was known for being home to the city's bohemians. In the late 1930s the first integrated nightclub in America, Café Society, had opened its doors in the neighborhood and was a place where Blacks, whites, and Latinos had applauded performances by Ella Fitzgerald, Billie Holiday, and, in later years, John Coltrane and Miles Davis. More recently the Beats had discovered the neighborhood: Allen Ginsberg and Jack Kerouac drank and smoked grass in scene bars like the White Horse Tavern alongside other famed writers like Truman Capote and Dylan Thomas. All this was enticing to Sidney Gottlieb: The people walking these streets were out for adventure—they were artists, intellectuals. This was an excellent place to secretly test LSD—not on his own colleagues or at universities, but out in the wild.

Located in the building at 81 Bedford Street was an apartment that two of his colleagues from the tech squad had equipped with microphones and cameras, several for still photographs as well as one movie camera. It was for them that Gottlieb was bringing the cash. The so-called safe house would be run by the equal parts jovial and brutal George Hunter White. Trained at Camp X, the British school for covert agents in Canada, where he had gotten to know Ian Fleming, future author of the James Bond novels, White had made a name for himself by shutting down the Hip Sing Tong brotherhood in Seattle—and was notorious for having strangled a Japanese agent in the middle of the street in Calcutta. Normally White worked for Anslinger's Federal Bureau of Narcotics, but Gottlieb borrowed him for this special operation, along with White's colleague Arthur Giuliani, who had returned to New York from Berlin. Gottlieb had gotten to know both men at the FBN's offices on Church Street in Lower Manhattan; afterward the two agents had completed a two-day crash course on all things LSD at the Roosevelt Hotel on Madison Avenue. The MK-Ultra chief had brought to this training session two dozen vials of the Sandoz drug to get the men ready for Bedford Street. A nine-page MK-Ultra memorandum describes the safe house as a soundproof setting, where the observation room especially should be as quiet as possible. "For technical reasons, it is best to have two adjoining rooms." The room in which the "activities" were to take place should have a "bed or studio couch or cot" and be large, since "a crowded room might produce confusion and hinder the development of the . . . technique." The adjoining room was "essential for the setting up of technical equipment, i.e., recording devices, transformers, etc.," and was intended "as an observation room and listening post for persons interested in the case to make notes or prepare questions" while the "activities" took place on the other side of the wall. A bathroom was also necessary in case water was needed or the techniques applied "produce[d] nausea, vomiting, or other conditions which [made] bathroom facilities essential."

White and Giuliani cruised around Greenwich Village and invited people they happened to meet to private parties at the apartment, where they secretly gave them LSD. Once responsible for drug *control* in occupied Berlin, Giuliani had now traded in his former brief for its exact opposite—and in so doing had what might have

"Here's looking at you, kid": pushing pills, CIA-style.

been an even more unusual experience than he'd had in bombed-out Berlin.

What exactly happened at the safe house remains shrouded in darkness to this day: All recordings and photographs made in the observation room were destroyed in 1973, when Richard Helms, Allen Dulles's successor as head of the CIA, ordered the destruction of the MK-Ultra files.* White's notebook survived and is today kept in the Stanford University archive. The entries inside are cryptic, the handwriting hard to read, as if White had written everything while intoxicated. "LSD surprise—can wash," reads one

---

* Nevertheless, 16,000 pages survived the records massacre, having been filed incorrectly and thus overlooked. Via the Freedom of Information Act they found their way to the author John Marks, who studied them for his authoritative work *The Search for the "Manchurian Candidate."*

entry for instance, possibly referring to the surprise that the involuntary user has in store for them, as well as touching on "brainwashing," the ultimate goal of the operation.

In order to make it easier for White and Giuliani and other MK-Ultra agents to secretly administer the drug, Gottlieb, as bizarre as it might sound, had gone looking for a magician. "We were casting about for a trustworthy person expert in magic," he recalled, "someone who knew sleight-of-hand well and who was well grounded, that was professional and . . . could interface well with our people and the narcotics officials working with us . . . We interviewed a number of subjects around the country, finding nobody really satisfactory."

Eventually the recruiting effort bore fruit and the spy agency hired the illusionist John Mulholland, who was famous throughout the country. In a conference room on the third floor of the elegant Statler Hotel at Thirty-Fourth Street and Seventh Avenue in Manhattan (the same hotel where Frank Olson had fallen to his death from a tenth-floor window; the CIA liked to use it because it was centrally located and anonymous), the magician held his first CIA seminar in June 1953 on the subject of "tricks with pills, liquids, and loose solids." Arthur Giuliani was among those who attended the course. Mulholland, whose wife was a relative of the future first lady Barbara Bush, had written a handbook for the occasion with the title "Some Operational Applications of the Art of Deception." The 120-page guide began with an "Introduction and General Comments on the Art of Deception" and went on to cover such disparate topics as the "Surreptitious Removal of Objects" and "Special Objects of Deception for Women." Mulholland supplemented his lessons with drawings he made himself.

Thus prepared, Gottlieb and Anslinger's agents went to set up a second safe house on K Street in Washington, DC, just around the corner from the State Department in a part of town favored by lobbyists. Meanwhile a separate observation site popped up on Maryland's Eastern Shore, on a farm not far from the small town of Easton. MK-Ultra now had three areas of American society covered: New York bohemia, the political power center of the capital, and suburbia. "Our studies of unconventional warfare have included for some time the potential agent LSD, which appears to be better adapted than known drugs to both interrogation of prisoners and use against troops or civilians," a CIA memorandum stated. Unwitting tests were conducted in order to explore the full spectrum of the operative use of LSD. Both questioning and the provocation of erratic behavior were of interest. "As a rule, individuals subjected to [these] techniques will be entirely co-operative."

Additional safe houses were planned for Chicago and other cities. Gottlieb also set his sights on the West Coast. There he undertook a targeted assault on the intimate lives of his fellow citizens. Again White acted as henchman: at 225 Chestnut Street in the Telegraph Hill neighborhood of San Francisco, under the pseudonym Morgan Hall, he rented an L-shaped apartment referred to internally as "the pad." He had a technology expert from UC Berkeley fit the place out with four high-quality DD4-Telefunken microphones—fine German workmanship—disguised as wall outlets and hooked up to two Model F-301 cassette recorders. For the furnishings of this apartment with sweeping views of San Francisco Bay, Alcatraz, and the Golden Gate Bridge, White drew inspiration from interiors he'd seen in *Playboy* magazine: shag carpets, Toulouse-Lautrec prints on the red-painted walls, low cocktail tables, a generously sized bed with a giant mirror on the wall. The "listening post" was located on the other side of the mirror and was equipped with a mobile toilet, which the pragmatic White used as a seat; a refrigerator, which he always kept stocked with a supply of martinis, was within reaching distance. On the walls of the observation room he hung posters showing "manacled women being tortured and whipped."

In order to lure subjects to the pad, "individuals at all social levels, high and low, native Americans and foreign," the agents used prostitutes—"certain individuals who covertly administer this material to other people in accordance with [White's] instructions," as Gottlieb wrote in his bone-dry bureaucratese.

The lives of others: secret LSD during an assignation.

The women received a hundred dollars, plus the money they got from the john, for each operation, though Gottlieb had to tie himself in knots trying to explain the missing receipts to CIA administrators: "Due to the highly unorthodox nature of these activities and the considerable risk incurred by these individuals, it is impossible to require that they provide a receipt for these payments or that they indicate the precise manner in which the funds were spent." The bookkeepers had to content themselves with voided checks that White had made out to "Stormy," one of his code words for LSD, or, clumsily, to "Undercover Agent." Every now and then he also used the code name for the safe house program in San Francisco: Operation Midnight Climax.

In order to fit in with the scene, for his missions on the West Coast the stocky White wore suede shoes, hats with wide, turned-up brims, and gaudy zircon rings. Thus turned out, he set forth to answer the question "How do you take a woman who is willing to use her body to get money out of a guy to get things which are much more important, like state secrets?" Where at first he had thought that the ideal time to find out something from a client was right *before* an approaching climax, the tests showed that this was rather a moment that the prostitutes could use to sell additional services. The opportunity for pillow talk had not yet arrived. In these moments, "the guy was focused solely on hormonal needs. He was not thinking of his career or anything else." It was far better to go to work *after* the sex, to wait until the postcoital cigarette was lit. "Most men who go to prostitutes are prepared for the fact that [after the act] she's beginning to work to get herself out of there, so she can get back on the street to make some more money . . . To find a prostitute who is willing to stay is a hell of a shock to anyone used to prostitutes. It has a tremendous effect on the guy. It's a boost to his ego if she's telling him he was really neat, and she wants to stay for a few more hours . . . Most of the time, he gets pretty vulnerable. What the hell's he going to talk about? Not the sex, so he starts talking about his business. It's at this time she can lead him gently."

To this day it is unclear how many people were unwittingly drugged or otherwise manipulated, and with what long-term consequences. George Hunter White summed up the approach in characteristically cynical terms: "Where else could a red-blooded American boy lie, kill, cheat, steal, rape, and pillage with the sanction and blessing of the All-Highest?"

Analyzing the intimate data was of importance to Gottlieb on two levels: For one, it had direct application in the conflict of the Cold War, which didn't stop at the bedroom door. In the divided Berlin of the 1960s, for example, the CIA ran a network of prostitutes to get at information on the Russian side. More than that, however, Gottlieb was interested in something deeper. As one of his colleagues later put it: "We learned a lot about human nature in the bedroom." As perverse as the experiments at the safe houses seem, they were fully in line with everything else Gottlieb was doing. The CIA was building an observation regime, a world of control facilitated by the consumption of substances that the consumers themselves weren't informed of. At Gottlieb's safe houses, people were supposed to relax and think they were enjoying their free time, having a nice drink with some new friends. In reality they were dosed with substances they didn't even know existed and then spied on—their behavior, what they said, their feelings and preferences all recorded. Through his actions the head of MK-Ultra had monopolized LSD. By sending his agents to pay a visit to Sandoz he had scuppered the possibility of its being distributed as a medication; by exerting his influence on the "subprojects" at the universities and institutes he instrumentalized, he had bent research into human consciousness to his own purposes.

Things didn't look good as far as drawing out the healing potential of LSD was concerned. But then something happened in a tiny mountain village in Mexico that once again changed everything.

PART III

N A R C O T I C

23

MÖSCH-RÜMMS

THREE THOUSAND MILES SOUTH OF NEW YORK AND A MILE above sea level lies the town of Huautla de Jiménez, where every year, at the beginning of the rainy season in early summer, mushrooms poke their light brown heads out of the earth. For generations they served as the only pharmaceutical in this place so long shut off from the outside world. They were used to treat all manner of ailments, whether it was broken bones, headaches, a bad flu, or memory loss in old age. Traditionally it wasn't the patient who took the mushrooms, but the doctor, who reportedly would receive suggestions from the mushrooms on how to treat the ailment. In the sixteenth century the Spanish missionary and Dominican friar Bernardino de Sahagún had become the first person outside of Huautla de Jiménez to give an account of *teonanacatl,* the "god mushroom." The Spanish colonial rulers didn't investigate the phenomenon any further; they wrote it off as superstition and remained convinced of the superiority of their own methods of healing. Besides, they were there for gold and to root out the natives' rites, not to study and preserve them.

For a long time the tradition had continued on in silence, at least as far as the outside world was concerned. The indigenous peoples of Mexico hadn't advertised it for fear of further persecution. Only in 1922 did Blasius Paul Reko, an Austrian conducting ethnobotanical research in the southern state of Oaxaca, come upon the god mushroom, which was supposed to give clairvoyant capabilities to those who ate it and enable them, as he described it, "to locate stolen property" and "air secrets." Thirty years later, Valentina and Gordon Wasson, a married couple living in New York who had devoted themselves to mycology and were working on an authoritative book on fungi, stumbled upon Reko's writings. Valentina Wasson was a pediatrician, her husband a vice president at J.P. Morgan Bank. He managed to get in touch with Reko by letter, and shortly before the Austrian's death he wrote back and in shaky handwriting tipped Gordon Wasson off to the mysterious happenings in the remote mountain region.

Having drummed up the necessary funding for an expedition, the Wassons, thanks to Gordon's professional connections, were even able to make use of the Banco Nacional de México's company plane, which took them as far as the Oaxacan state capital of Oaxaca de Juárez. After that the journey continued by donkey. In Huautla they gave the top official in town a watch, the children crayons, and went to see several healers, known as *curanderos*. To their disappointment, no one they spoke to would furnish them with a sufficient amount of the specimens they sought. Only in subsequent years, on his third visit to the mountain village, did Gordon Wasson meet a middle-aged woman of short stature named Maria Sabina who didn't set store by the traditional rite, in which only the *curandero* ingested the mushroom. Sabina wasn't known in the village as a healer, but she knew where to find the cowpats from which the little toadstools sprouted. The price she demanded was steep: one hundred pesos (about eighty dollars in 1955), one chicken, two chicken eggs, one turkey egg, copal incense, two candles made of beeswax, two parrot feathers, and a few sheets of paper. For this princely sum, Sabina was prepared to supply a strong gringo dose.

What happened that night was as extraordinary as it was consequential. In her thatched-roof adobe hut, Maria Sabina served the mushrooms to the Wall Street banker and his travel companion, a photographer who usually made his money documenting jet-set weddings. Then she started singing village songs in her native tongue of Mixeteco. Her two daughters posed and preened in the light of the camera's flash, and over the next few hours they all celebrated a supposedly ancient ritual that had never really existed. In reality they invented the trip. Sabina had gauged the dose right, because soon Wasson was flooded with visions "in vivid color, always harmonious" that "began with art motifs, angular such as might decorate carpets or textiles or wall-paper or the drawing board of an architect." Palaces formed beneath his eyelids, "resplendent palaces all laid over with semiprecious stones," with "courts, arcades, gardens" and "a mythological beast drawing a regal chariot." He saw "camel caravans advancing slowly across the slopes"; "river estuaries, pellucid water flowing through an endless expanse of reeds down to a measureless sea"; "a human figure appeared, a woman in primitive costume, standing and staring across the water." But the mushrooms didn't just bring on splendid visions; they had a pleasant physical effect as well and produced a feeling of well-being that lasted for hours. "Our trip this time has been successful beyond our dreams," Wasson wrote to his secretary in New York the next morning. "The effects of these mushrooms are beyond belief."

Back in his penthouse in Manhattan, Wasson went for a repeat performance with dried specimens that he'd brought back with him. He looked out at the treetops in Central Park. The effects were even stronger than in the adobe hut, and his record player was able to stand in for the live singing: "For the first time the word ecstasy took on real meaning." Wasson decided to write about his discovery. His fifteen-page account, complete with color photographs, appeared in the May 13, 1957, issue of the influential *Life* magazine, and with it the term "magic mushroom" also appeared for the first time. In his retelling, Wasson changed Maria Sabina's name to the biblically tinged Eva Mendez and described her as a shaman "of the highest quality," "a woman without stain . . . with a spirituality in her expression that struck us at once." The mushrooms he described as "sacred," himself and the photographer, not entirely accurately, as "the first white men in recorded history to eat the divine mushrooms, which for centuries have been a secret."

The article landed like a bombshell in America. Wasson's exoticizing presentation of Maria Sabina fascinated thousands of readers; they too wanted to be put in a trance and have divine experiences with the "Indians." Soon foreigners began traveling to Huautla in droves, upsetting the balance of the place, and Maria Sabina was ostracized in her own village. Her hut was even set on fire so that she would commit no more acts of "betrayal" of the "god mushroom." But the rush never abated. Even today, Huautla is strongly impacted by mushroom tourism.

What was in these unusual toadstools that produced the mystical experiences? Maria Sabina didn't know, and neither did Gordon Wasson. He began working with Professor Roger Heim, the world's leading mycologist and head of France's Muséum National d'Histoire Naturelle. In Paris Heim attempted to analyze the magic mushrooms, but without success. As Wasson wrote, "The mushrooms present a chemical problem. What is the agent in them that releases the strange hallucinations? . . . The chemist has a long road to go before he will isolate it, arrive at its molecular structure and synthesize it. The problem is of great interest in the realm of pure science. Will it also prove of help in coping with psychic disturbances?"

Now Albert Hofmann was contacted, because, he wrote, "the symptoms that set in after ingesting the mushrooms . . . [are] very much comparable with those that occurred with mescaline or our LSD substance." Heim traveled to Basel, gave a report at Sandoz headquarters "on the results of his research and his expedition to Mexico," and left his host, "right then and there," with "a small quantity of dried mushroom material . . . for experiments for orientation purposes," later on supplementing this with "32 dried specimens . . . which together weighed a total of 2.4 grams."

Hofmann described the effect of the "quite strong dose": "The world outside began to transform in an exotic manner. Everything took on a Mexican character." At first Hofmann thought he was

*Sandoz's psychedelic lab: happy Swiss chemists
with happy Mexican mushrooms (Albert Hofmann, right).*

imagining this effect, since after all he knew that the specimens
came from Mexico. He concentrated hard: "[I tried] to see the world
around me as I normally knew it. All the efforts of my will to see
things in their familiar shapes and colors were unsuccessful. With
my eyes open or closed, I saw only Indian motifs and colors"—in
the middle of Basel. When the company doctor leaned over him to
measure his blood pressure, "he transformed into an Aztec priest
performing a sacrifice." "I wouldn't have been surprised if he had
pulled out a knife made of obsidian. Despite the gravity of the situation it amused me to see how the Germanic face of my colleague had
taken on a purely Indian aspect."

Excited, Hofmann wrote his friend the writer Ernst Jünger, with
whom he had shared psychedelic experiences: "Now we are working on isolating the active principle. I'm curious if it's chemically
related to lysergic acid diethylamide."

The chemists at the Sandoz lab started putting in overtime—after
all, the competition had read the article in *Life* too. "In America the
Merck and SKF companies are pursuing chemical research into

Mexican mushrooms," a Sandoz memo noted. "It seems however that the material they have to work with is neither sufficient in quantity nor reliably verified." The researchers at Sandoz gained a crucial advantage by testing the psychoactivity of isolated components out on themselves rather than leave this to lab animals. To give the company lab the right ambience, Albert Hofmann took the extra step of having a stained-glass window put in. It depicted Asclepius, the ancient Greek god of medicine, next to his mentor, the centaur Chiron.

The support Hofmann summoned seemed to help. In early 1958, after more than a year of research, they'd done it: "The compounds whose wondrous effects led the Indians to believe for millennia that a god resided within the mushrooms had their chemical structures elucidated and could now be produced synthetically in the test-tube," Hofmann wrote proudly.

He dubbed the isolated alkaloid "psilocybin." In the *Deutsche Medizinischen Wochenschrift* his colleague Aurelio Cerletti, director of Sandoz's pharmacological laboratory, announced the "demystification of the ancient Aztec drug by means of modern science. The tiny mushrooms and the magic power contained within them [have been] wrested out of the darkness of centuries past and the influence of magical notions by joint ethnographic-mycological and chemical-pharmacological research."

The medication that Sandoz developed was called Indocybin. Each pill contained two milligrams of synthetic psilocybin. This helped, according to the drug information sheet, with "psychic relief in the treatment of neurosis," with compulsion and anxiety, hysteria, addiction, and depression. Psilocybin was also a significant component in the development of other compounds. In the years to come, Sandoz would use it to create the first beta-blockers: blood pressure-lowering drugs used to regulate heart function.

What delighted Hofmann the most about demystifying the magic mushroom was the molecular similarity between psilocybin and LSD. Both substances functioned in the brain in a similar way. LSD, that hard-to-understand, downright mysterious substance that was the cause of much dispute among psychiatrists and psychologists—and also, of course, among mind-manipulators—had now been given a colorful, innocent companion. The natural magic mushroom, this "dazzling relation loaded with exotic clichés," breathed new life into the semi-synthetic sac fungus product, took LSD under its gills and made it respectable. From that point on the two substances were seen as a pair, and if "Mösch-Rümms," as Hofmann lovingly dubbed the fungi in his Swiss accent, enabled, per *Life* magazine, a positive journey of self-discovery, then so would LSD.

Hofmann emerged highly motivated from his work on the new medicine and started thinking about whether it might be possible to produce a whole range of novel substances: "It seems that the clinical evaluation of other simple lysergic acid derivatives and relatives of LSD has a few more interesting things yet to yield." Conscious of the fact that he had "done pioneering work" at Sandoz, he proposed that the company devote itself to its self-professed "main focus of isolating the active agents in highly potent medicinal plants," which, he pointed out, had been "made the basis of our pharmaceutical division by Herr Professor Stoll." The chemist envisioned a complete reorientation of the company, which he saw as a future production site for psychedelic medicines—a logical extension of Stoll's original idea of harnessing the power of plants. What this would mean, he explained in his memo, would be to "make the study of drugs with effects on the psyche a special area of focus in our research plan. If additional therapeutically viable compounds with effects on the psyche could successfully be made available to the field of psychiatry, then the prestige that Sandoz already enjoys in this area will be solidified and enlarged. It seems to me that one especially important aspect of such a working plan would be to chemically modify the genuinely psychically active compounds in order to vary their effectiveness and toxicity . . . In so doing it could be possible to create new kinds of medicine."

But Stoll rejected the proposal outright. The substances were too volatile for the once "fearless" CEO. If the former pharma-pioneer had known that three-quarters of a century later start-up labs all over the world would be hard at work driving the development of psychedelic drugs forward in the hopes of reaping billions in profits, he might have arrived at a different decision.

But Stoll, who in all likelihood had never tried LSD himself, didn't realize the potential, which might just have made Sandoz the global market leader.

24

BULK ORDER

BY THE TIME THE *LIFE* ARTICLE CAME OUT, THE OLD LABEL "psychotomimetic" had outlived its usefulness. When, over the course of their correspondence, Aldous Huxley and the British psychiatrist Humphry Osmond tried to come up with a name for the new kind of consciousness-altering drugs, Osmond offered a suggestion in doggerel form: "To fathom Hell or go angelic / Just take a pinch of *psychedelic*." The name stuck, and from that point forward *psychedelics* enjoyed growing popularity, the experiences they unleashed considered by more and more and more people to be "the best and clearest path ever discovered to self-acceptance and self-understanding."

This development caught Gottlieb wrong-footed, given that it was diametrically opposed to his idea of deploying LSD as a weapon. The head of MK-Ultra also had a copy of *Life* magazine on his desk, and that was no coincidence. Those who read Gordon Wasson's enthusiastic article through to the end would have seen Wasson's grateful acknowledgment of his financial supporters in the final paragraph. The CIA might not have been listed among them, but a "Geschickter Fund for Medical Research" was, and it happened to be one of the foundations that Gottlieb used to inconspicuously channel funds to projects that, in exchange, sent him their findings. But even if he had been kept extensively informed about Wasson's expeditions, what good did it do him? Pandora's box had been opened; the mushroom boom, and the LSD boom with it, seemed unstoppable. Even Hollywood celebrities joined in, bringing with them the strong influence they exerted on American public opinion. Magic mushrooms and LSD became the talk of Tinseltown as stars and starlets were introduced to the drugs on their psychiatrists' couches. The urbane Cary Grant, for three decades one of the biggest actors in Hollywood, with appearances in countless comedies and thrillers and starring roles in Hitchcock classics like *North by Northwest*, was so impressed by his more than sixty experiences with the Sandoz drug that he started raving about it. "All my life," he told reporters, "I've been searching for peace of mind. I'd explored yoga and hypnotism and made several attempts at mysticism. Nothing really seemed to give me what I wanted until this treatment." On another occasion he remarked, "I don't actually like drugs, but LSD did me a lot of good. I think all politicians should take it."

More and more influential people experienced the drug for themselves. One of them was Al Hubbard, a businessman who had made his fortune in uranium and had once been an agent for the disbanded OSS military intelligence agency, though he held no truck with its successor: "The CIA work stinks." The well-connected Hubbard believed strongly in LSD as a "mystical" medicine and wanted to distribute it extensively among the movers and shakers of the country on account of its psychotherapeutic potential. With this aim in mind he purchased from Sandoz "43 boxes of L.S.D., 25 ampoules per box." In his private plane he flew around America with little more in his suitcase than a few clean shirts and a supply of LSD. "If you don't think it's amazing, all I've got to say is just go ahead and try it" was the standard pitch he gave before sending another senator, tycoon, entertainer, or sports legend off on a massive trip—down a few hundred micrograms, then see what happens.

But Hubbard wasn't the biggest advocate for the new psychedelic movement. This distinction belonged to Timothy Leary, a Harvard professor and former West Point cadet trained as a psychologist who wore his hair in a crew cut and always dressed in either a corduroy jacket or buttoned-up gray flannel suit—the perfect 1950s son-in-law. Leary had written a psychology textbook that was well received by his peers and had also developed a personality test, known immodestly as "the Leary," that was used by, among others, the CIA to evaluate potential new hires. The proper prof had had nothing to do with drugs until the summer of 1960, when, while on vacation in Mexico, a friend had given him a handful of mushrooms that he'd gotten from an old indigenous woman. Leary hesitated for a while but then, not wanting to offend his friend, washed them down with Carta Blanca rum. What happened next had consequences for the subsequent course of American history. "It was above all and without question the deepest religious experience of my life," Leary recounted. "I discovered that beauty, revelation, sensuality . . . all lie inside my body, outside my mind."

Back at Harvard, Leary, with the blessing of the president of the Department of Social Relations, set up a "Psilocybin Project" that made it possible for students and Leary's fellow professors to test the substance in an academic environment and study its effects on the psyche. In no time Leary went from being known as a bore to becoming the most popular professor at the school. "You can be a convict or a college professor," he euphorically proclaimed, "you'll still have a mystical, transcendental experience." After the claustrophobic fifties with its friend-or-foe mindset, it was time to cultivate visions, to offer a new metaphysics that would imbue life in society with meaning again. According to Leary the dominant drugs alcohol and caffeine exerted a constraining influence on the neurological connections in the brain: "Politics, religion, economics, social structure, are based on shared states of consciousness. The cause of social conflict is usually neurological. The cure is biochemical."

From then on the professor started telling everyone about psychedelic substances and eagerly handing them out. When Allen Ginsberg showed up at Leary's house, the influential Beat poet was so taken with the magic mushrooms that he took his clothes off and tried to go running through the streets of Boston to deliver the good news to everyone. "We're going to teach people to stop hating," Ginsberg proclaimed. "[We'll] start a peace and love movement." When Leary held him back—it was winter and freezing cold outside—Ginsberg grabbed the nearest telephone and tried to call the US president, the general secretary of the USSR, and Mao Zedong. When he couldn't get through to the decision-makers he called his buddy Jack Kerouac instead and woke him up. Kerouac, author of the counterculture classic *On the Road*, had to promise Ginsberg that in the future he would take psychedelics instead of speed. Of his first trip, which he took at his mother's house, Kerouac reported: "Mainly I felt like a floating Khan on a magic carpet with my interesting lieutenants and gods ... We were at the extremist point goofing at clouds watching the movie of existence ... Everybody seemed innocent ... It was a definite Satori. Full of psychic clairvoyance . . . The faculty of remembering names and what one has learned is heightened so fantastically that we could develop the greatest scholars and scientists in the world with this stuff."

Encouraged by reactions such as these, Leary placed a bulk order with Sandoz: one hundred grams of LSD and twenty-five kilograms of psilocybin—enough to send about two million Americans on a trip. The Swiss were jubilant. To that point Sandoz had seen hardly any revenue from the psychedelic medicine, but had sunk a lot of money into research and development. Now they had an order valued at close to two million Swiss francs. Albert Hofmann especially felt a sense of gratification. The reaction at Sandoz's British affiliate L. Light and Co., which had received Leary's order, was more restrained, however. The company's representative wrote to the Harvard professor saying that they were "fascinated with the scope that your proposed new task will take in" but requested "a little more information on your plans. Is your project dependent on a U.S. Government Contract given by one of the Armed Forces or the Food and Drug Administration in Washington, or does the money come from an organisation such as the Ford Foundation?" The company wanted to make sure that the project was being carried out with "the support and full cognisance of some department of the U.S. Government." Once again the Faustian bargain that Stoll had made with Gottlieb ten years earlier came back to bite him. In his reply Leary claimed vaguely that he was in touch with those responsible at the FDA. These contacts had promised him, he said, that the packages would clear customs if they bore the following advisory: "CAUTION: New Drug Limited by Federal Law for Investigational Use."

To see to it that the lucrative deal didn't fall through—a deal that would have bolstered his own reputation as well—Albert Hofmann got personally involved. On January 24 he wrote to Leary that he had "followed with great interest" his Psilocybin Project and had been apprised of his interest in ordering such "appreciable amounts" in connection with it. For Hofmann the order from the elite university must have represented a suitable reward for all his efforts. He assured the prospective major customer that the sales division would be sending him a quote in a separate letter: "It would give me great pleasure if our firm could supply the substances for your research project." Sandoz sent the sales quote to Boston that same day: for twenty-five kilograms of psilocybin, "the factory" asked 75 Swiss francs per gram for a total of 1,875,000 CHF. The LSD was priced at 508 francs per gram, adding an additional 50,800 francs to the order, with a delivery time of "within about 3–4 weeks." Leary, the letter advised, should enclose with his order confirmation of the "import license issued by your competent authorities according to the new regulations referring to such drugs." "You may be assured," the letter from Basel continued, "that we shall not fail to do all in our power in order to satisfy you in every respect and thanking you in anticipation for your further news, we remain, Gentlemen, Yours very truly, Sandoz LTD."

Not everyone at the company was so cooperative. A few days later, on January 29, 1963, at four-thirty p.m., Yves Dunant, Sandoz's new general director and successor to the now retired Arthur Stoll, had a phone call with his US subsidiary, during which he was "warned against sending the amount ordered. A letter from Dr. Henze will arrive next week with the necessary explanations."

Henze, who already had cold feet where LSD was concerned, had become even less sanguine in the past few years. In 1962 investigators from the Food and Drug Administration had paid an unannounced visit to his office, which had since moved to New Jersey, looked through all the files from the last five years and demanded "copies of all correspondence dealing with LSD and psilocybin." "Of all drugs that we know about," a letter from the FDA stated, "[there are] none which deserve controlled handling to a greater extent than these." In Henze, the head of Sandoz's New York office, the American government officials had found a man they could trust. "We appreciate very much the cooperative attitude that your firm has shown . . . in connection with an extensive investigation we have been making of LSD-25, psilocybin and other hallucinatory drugs. We have received the many files that you furnished."

Sandoz was given an acknowledgment that its "slate was clean," as Henze proudly informed Dunant. And to make sure it stayed that way, he warned his boss "that henceforth the F.D.A. would be increasingly alert to what was being done with these compounds," since "it had transpired that an illicit traffic in LSD and other hallucinogenic compounds has been under way in various parts of the country." Henze became even more explicit: "Certain groups outside of the medical field have been playing around with hallucinogenic substances and . . . the drug has also found its way into the hands of drug addicts and other fringes of psychopathic personality groups." With regard to Leary's order, Henze believed that "the quantities of LSD and psilocybin to be quoted on are completely unrealistic and in the hands of these people would have to be considered a danger to public health aside from a violation of the laws."

Henze's colleague Albert Hofmann became a target of his accusations. Henze judged Hofmann's letter to Leary "extremely compromising." It made his own assurances to the FDA that Sandoz would maintain strict controls over the consciousness-altering substances seem unreliable. Henze warned that as a result of Hofmann's actions Sandoz had opened itself up to criminal investigations, including the potential arrest of certain employees should they visit the United States. As for Leary himself, Henze cast doubt on his being a "bona fide researcher" and assured the head of the company that Harvard University didn't approve of its professor's order. Sure, Leary was still a member of the school's faculty and could use its letterhead: "We know, however, that Leary has been fired because of his and his associates' irresponsible manner in which he has used halluci-nogenic substances [*sic*]. In any case, the university has completely distanced itself from these individuals."

Who was the "we" that the former Alsos agent was referring to here? He wrote this letter on February 7, 1963, when Leary was still on the payroll in Cambridge. How was it that the head of Sandoz's American subsidiary was so well informed about the strictly con-fidential goings-on at Harvard? The renowned institution hadn't fired a single professor throughout that whole century. All the Sandoz executives knew was that the university was secretly gath-ering evidence against the popular teacher. On February 1, Harvard had sent a telegram to Basel with the request that Sandoz send a copy of Leary's order. Disregarding any discretion they might owe toward their prospective customer, the pharma concern complied with the request. Even Albert Hofmann, who could sense the shift in the wind, now expressed "serious doubts . . . as to whether the substances in question could ever be supplied."

Unconcerned, Leary confirmed his order. He couldn't include the import permit as stipulated. Instead he enclosed a check for ten thousand dollars as a down payment, repeating his request that the packages be labeled "CAUTION: New Drug Limited by Federal Law for Investigational Use" and writing, "We have assurance that pack-ages so addressed and labeled will be cleared by customs and F.D.A." "*Was heißt das?*," Hofmann noted in pencil in the margin of the let-ter: "What does that mean?" And there was another thing that both-ered the Swiss chemist, namely Leary's proud mention of the news that journalists would be writing about his research plans. Far from impressing Hofmann, this kind of PR flew in the face of the serious science that was so dear to his heart. "Apparently that's the most important thing!" he wrote again in the margin, and in a reply expressed his regret toward Leary's enthusiasm for the media, "which [could] only be injurious to the scientific clarification of questions connected with the use of these substances."

In order to assure himself of the seriousness of his prospective customer, and hoping to save what at this point was all but past saving, Hofmann wrote to his friend and correspondent Aldous Huxley and asked his opinion of Leary. The writer answered right away: He too had been "annoyed & disturbed by the stupid and sensational publicity surrounding LSD." But he came to the defense of Leary, whom he had known for years, and praised his "very valuable pioneering work." Of the group experiments at Harvard he had gotten the impression that "the results have been very interesting and, for many individuals, spiritually fruitful." His response echoed an earlier letter in which he wrote of Leary's projects, "I have good hopes that this and similar work will result in the development of a real Natural History of visionary experience . . . & at the same time of a technique of 'Applied Mysticism'—a technique for helping individuals to get the most out of their transcendental experience and to make use of their insights from the 'other world' in the affairs of 'this world.'" Concluding his March 1963 letter, Huxley wrote, "I hope very much that all the difficulties will soon be cleared up and that all the American workers [researchers] . . . will be able to get the necessary materials."

This made Hofmann feel better at least, but at Sandoz the decision had already been made. The sales division politely thanked Leary, but regretted "not being able to accept this order." The check was duly returned.

In an act of desperation Leary flew from Boston to New Jersey to try to convince Henze in person. Years later, the latter described the meeting: "We were the only source back then, and there was a big demand . . . I had to be very careful, the FDA and the like were after us and demanded reliable paperwork. All Leary had was talk . . . I inquired at Harvard by telephone, the answer on that point was not satisfying, because Leary wanted to use students for his experiments . . . Then it turned into a big drama, the government (FDA) got involved in every project. You had to be a big player to get permission to work with the stuff. Leary was dissatisfied and incautious. . . . I actually didn't think he was 'malign,' just incompetent. A windbag."

Disappointed, Leary went back to Boston. Now he was stuck without a supplier. Nevertheless he tried to continue his experiments—and walked right into a trap. It didn't take long for the first black market LSD to reach campus by way of Harvard Square. Things had now escalated to a whole new level. Some of the school's leading dignitaries spoke out against their colleague. Henry K. Beecher, who not long before then had been restaging Nazi drug experiments at the university hospital, warned of the alleged health risks of LSD, and in the *Boston Globe* the Harvard professor Max Rinkel claimed that the substances triggered a chemical reaction in the brain whose terrible effects might last for months after use. Leary cuttingly shot back: "LSD is a psychedelic drug which occasionally causes psychotic behavior in people who have NOT taken it." Instead of dialing back, he doubled down and started inviting Psilocybin Project participants to parties at his house. Thumbing his nose at the prudery of the American way of life, he declared that taking psychedelics was sexually liberating as well: Women could have "several hundred orgasms" while on the drugs, he proclaimed, full of bluster, in an interview with *Playboy*. Huxley, who also lived in Boston, warned his psychedelic brother-in-arms, "We've stirred up enough trouble suggesting that drugs can stimulate aesthetic and religious experiences. I strongly urge you not to let the sexual cat out of the bag."

And Huxley wasn't the only advocate of consciousness exploration who felt that Leary's enthusiasm, frequently combined with exaggerated self-promotion, went too far. Others in the movement feared that he was putting their own studies at risk, that his flamboyant demeanor was utterly discrediting the idea of LSD as a tool.

He was "making [their] work far harder." Al Hubbard voiced his displeasure: "He seemed like a well-intentioned person, but then he went overboard." The British scientist Humphry Osmond shared the sentiments of his friend Huxley, who was "genuinely concerned and afraid that Timothy's excess of enthusiasm may do much harm."

25

LSDJFK

ONE OF LEARY'S MOST EXPLOSIVE CONTACTS TOOK PLACE when he looked up from his desk one day and saw a "woman leaning against the door post" of his Harvard office, "hip tilted provocatively," as he described it with chauvinistic flare in his autobiography. "She appeared to be in her late thirties. Good looking. Flamboyant eyebrows, piercing green-blue eyes, fine-boned face. Amused, arrogant, aristocratic."

"Dr. Leary, I've got to talk to you," the woman said by way of greeting. She walked toward him and shook his hand. "I'm Mary Pinchot. I've come from Washington to discuss something very important. I want to learn how to run an LSD session."

"That's our specialty here," Leary replied. "Would you like to tell me what you have in mind?"

"I have this friend who's a very important man. He's impressed by what I've told him about my own LSD experiences and what other people have told him. He wants to try it himself. So I'm here to learn how to do it."

"Why don't you have your important friend come here with you?" asked Leary, whose interest was piqued.

"Out of the question," said the visitor. "My friend is a public figure. It's just not possible."

Mary Pinchot came from an influential East Coast family; her husband of many years, whom she had divorced, was Cord Meyer, who led the CIA's Operation Mockingbird, which sought to infiltrate domestic and international media institutions. Pinchot was different. As an avowed pacifist, a journalist, and a painter, her activities in Washington made her what today would be called an influencer. In the capital's innermost circles the passionate supporter of a policy of détente was known for her close friendship with John F. Kennedy. There was a rumor that the two of them had smoked marijuana at the White House, where she "was almost part of the furniture." Even when official business was being discussed, the president didn't ask her to leave the room, "unlike with some of the other women—and men."

In April 1963 Pinchot encouraged Kennedy to order a unilateral stop to nuclear testing and not allow himself to get into a "pissing contest" with the Russians, among other things. Suddenly the president who had gone through the Cuban Missile Crisis and was known as a supporter of arms buildup took on a new tone, and on June 10, 1963, at American University gave what came to be known as his "Peace Speech." In it he expressed skepticism toward the policy of spending billions of dollars to maintain a nuclear deterrence capability. Every individual "who despair[ed] of war and wishe[d] to bring peace" needed to "begin by looking inward": "Our problems are manmade—therefore, they can be solved by man. And man can be as big as he wants." The person at the head of the American government sounded like a hippie: "For, in the final analysis, our most basic common link is that we all inhabit this small planet. We all breathe the same air. We all cherish our children's future. And we are all mortal."

Half a year later bullets fired from the dark recesses of the American state apparatus mangled the brain in which such a reversal in thinking seemed to have begun. Neither did Mary Pinchot survive the revanchist backlash. Ten months after the murder of the man rumored to be her lover, she too became the victim of an assassination. While walking on the towpath of the Chesapeake and Ohio Canal near her Georgetown apartment she was, it is no exaggeration to say, executed, shot twice in the head and back under circumstances that still today have yet to be explained. That same day, her diary was stolen from her bedroom.

26

THE REVOLT OF THE GUINEA PIGS

WHEN, IN MAY 1963, BLACK-MARKET LSD ONCE AGAIN TURNED up at Harvard, this time in the possession of a freshman student, it was the last straw. The administration held Leary responsible, presented him with a list of alleged transgressions, and dismissed him and his fellow professor Richard Alpert from their positions, stopping payment on their salaries with retroactive effect going back to April 30. In the student newspaper, the *Harvard Crimson,* the two fired academics were described as "spreading infection" and the university praised for putting a stop to the unorthodox consciousness research. Leary derided the elite university and declared that LSD was "more important than Harvard."

Choosing to regard his dismissal as a moment of liberation, the ex-professor concentrated his efforts on his private research institute, the International Federation for Internal Freedom. Together with his followers, he continued to conduct his studies at a beach hotel in Mexico, then at a patron's estate in Millbrook, New York. When America attacked North Vietnam on August 5, 1964, and launched one of the bloodiest wars of the twentieth century, he aligned himself with the peace movement. Leary proposed the mass intake of LSD as a way of ending a way of life geared toward confrontation, and thus solving all the world's problem. He boiled down his instructions for political action to a concise formula: *Turn on, tune in, drop out.* Soon LSD and Leary were being mentioned in the same breath. The press was writing about the substance in almost exclusively negative terms: LSD made you crazy, caused chromosomal damage and even leukemia, led to birth defects, homosexuality, and blindness, caused brain damage, and generally changed the user's character for the worse. "Girl, 5, Eats LSD and Goes Wild!," ran a typical headline from those days.

Word of the consciousness-altering power of the molecule spread all throughout the land, and on the West Coast in particular. For this Sidney Gottlieb was responsible, albeit involuntarily. In 1960, at Veteran Hospital in Menlo Park, California, in the heart of what is now Silicon Valley, a burly young man with blue eyes took part in a series of experiments sponsored by MK-Ultra. Ken Kesey was paid seventy-five dollars for his first LSD trip, and it wouldn't be his last. While tripping, Kesey, who was interested in psychiatry, believed that for the first time he understood the phenomena of "insanity" and "psychosis": "Before I took drugs, I didn't know why the guys at the psycho ward at the VA hospital were there. After I took LSD, suddenly I saw it. I saw it all. I listened to them and watched them, and I saw that what they were saying and doing was not so crazy after all." On another trip Kesey had a vision of a schizophrenic Native American with a "primitive" face. He decided his name was Chief Broom and made him the narrator of his first novel, *One Flew Over the Cuckoo's Nest*. The book became a global bestseller and was made into a film with Jack Nicholson—who often took LSD himself—in the leading role. Kesey used the royalties to buy a three-acre estate covered in redwoods in La Honda, an hour's drive south of San Francisco. There the writer threw LSD parties, which were written about both by Tom Wolfe in *The Electric Kool-Aid Acid Test* and Hunter S. Thompson in *Fear and Loathing in Las Vegas*. Kesey gave up writing books in 1964 and devoted himself exclusively to the new movement. Determined to spread the word to the world at large, he bought an old school bus, painted it in bright colors, and christened it "Furthur." In his bus he careened around the country and introduced more Americans to LSD than anyone else. He called his mission "the revolt of the guinea pigs."

John Lennon once reflected on the unplanned result of Sidney Gottlieb's efforts, LSD's mutation from instrument of mind control to recreational drug: "We must always remember to thank the CIA and the Army for LSD ... They brought out LSD to control people, and what they did was give us freedom." The music of the Beatles changed decisively after he and George Harrison were served espresso with LSD-laced sugar cubes after a dinner with their dentist in London. "I had such an overwhelming feeling of well-being, that there was a God, and I could see him in every blade of grass," Harrison remembered. "It was like gaining hundreds of years of experience in twelve hours." They rode out the trip at Harrison's house: "God, it was just terrifying," John recalled, "but it was fantastic, George's house seemed to be just like a big submarine." The LSD experience transformed the Beatles into boundary-pushing avant-garde musicians and inspired, for starters, the album *Revolver*, featuring the distinctly hypnotic song "Tomorrow Never Knows," which begins with two lines from the *Tibetan Book of the Dead* that John had come across in Timothy Leary's book *The Psychedelic Experience*: "Turn off your mind / Relax, and float downstream." Paul McCartney confirmed that LSD "started to find its way into everything we did, really. It colored our perceptions. I think we started to realize there wasn't [*sic*] as many frontiers as we'd thought there were. And we realized we could break barriers."

More and more influential musicians started using LSD as creative fuel. Bob Dylan went from being a guitar-strumming folk singer to a genius bursting the bounds of the culture; Jimi Hendrix turned on his amp, tuned his guitar, and dropped acid at the Woodstock Festival, where he played the National Anthem as it had never been played before. In San Francisco, where not long before then George Hunter White had been slipping LSD into people's cocktails without their knowledge, an entire neighborhood, Haight-Ashbury, came to be oriented around one thing: taking as much LSD as possible and getting as far away as possible from the racist, sexist America of the Cold War—a war that, due to Vietnam, had turned hot. Hundreds of thousands took part in happenings, tripping collectively for days and nights at a time. A counterculture took hold of every aspect of life in society, leaving its mark on music, fashion, film, consumer behavior, relationship models. There was no stopping the spread of the virus that was LSD. Those who had been infected were considered *experienced*, and had access to spaces that the *inexperienced* couldn't imagine. Suddenly in California you could surf on more than just the waves of the Pacific Ocean; now you could surf the waves of your own consciousness, too.

Skeptical voices were also heard. William Burroughs, drug doyen and mentor to the Beats, certainly had nothing against dropping out, but insisted more on the right "to withdraw from a social environment that offers no spiritual sustenance." He also conceded that psychedelics opened the doors of perception, as Huxley had postulated. But, said the author of *Naked Lunch*, only the careful cultivation of new forms of consciousness and modes of behavior would imbue visionary experiences with lasting significance. Where the psychedelic movement was concerned, Burroughs remained wary. He warned that people in search of meaning were susceptible to manipulation. Sour and stinging, he got right to the point within the first few pages of his novel *Nova Express*: "Flush their drug kicks down the drain—*They are poisoning and monopolizing the hallucinogen drugs—learn to make it without any chemical corn.*" The music icon Frank Zappa couldn't join in on the enthusiasm either and spoke of the rift that was forming between hippies who wanted to explore their minds and political radicals who were striving to change society along socialist lines: "The whole 'mind expansion' hype had been a clever ploy by the CIA on behalf of the entire Western establishment to undermine the potential threat of the emerging youth culture." Those who took LSD focused less on Karl Marx, more on Groucho.

For the American government, however, the promiscuous use of a substance that altered perception and put strange thoughts into the minds of the youth served as a reason to tighten the laws yet again. With the Drug Abuse Control Amendments of 1965, endorsed by President Lyndon B. Johnson as a measure "to protect the public health and safety," psychedelic substances were criminalized for the first time. The FDA withdrew approval for the use of LSD and psilocybin in psychotherapy. On October 6, 1966, LSD was declared an illegal substance in the United States and subsequently added to the United Nations' "Single Convention on Narcotic Drugs" promoted by Harry J. Anslinger since the late 1940s, which meant a worldwide ban. LSD was classified, along with heroin, as a schedule 1 drug— "No currently accepted medical use"—and subject to the most strict level of regulation. All of a sudden the substance was considered so dangerous that it was illegal even to do research into whether this was actually true—a prohibitionary Catch-22.

Sandoz dutifully recalled all samples that had been sent to therapists and researchers. Even before the ban went into effect internationally, the company once more went above and beyond: "This decision however applies not only to the United States, but was intended by Sandoz to apply to all other countries as well, including Switzerland." All non-military research projects at universities around the world were halted. The consciousness researcher Humphry Osmond had earlier spoken of a "fantastic lack of a coherent and sensible policy" at Sandoz, where the remaining supply was kept in a refrigerator that was chained shut. Every few weeks an inspector came and weighed everything to make sure that no one had been illicitly helping themselves to the LSD. In consequence, ergot cultivation in the Emmental and the backcountry outside of Lucerne also suffered. The farmers there gradually switched to growing beans and strawberries.

What Anslinger and Giuliani had wanted to achieve after the war in bombed-out Berlin had become global reality two decades later. A unified regulatory regime, put into effect by the United Nations, outlawed a range of substances and active ingredients, and included among them was the former potential miracle medicine from Switzerland.

27

THE BEAR

PROHIBITION DIDN'T MEAN A DROP IN DEMAND. WHO WOULD produce LSD from now on in sufficient quantities and equal in quality to Albert Hofmann's product? The ability and ethos of underground chemists would be crucial. The demand was massive, and the need was growing.

The thirty-year-old artist Owsley Stanley, grandson of a former Kentucky governor, decided to solve the problem himself. He acquired the necessary know-how in chemistry on his own, with the help of his girlfriend, who was trained in the field, and books from the public library. You just had to be diligent about it, he said of his do-it-yourself method. In Richmond, California, not far from San Francisco, he made pills he dubbed White Lightning, containing 270 micrograms each, then moved production to Denver, where he synthesized the substance with 99 percent purity, a quality that supposedly surpassed that of Albert Hofmann's product. Over many years Sandoz had produced 400 grams of LSD, four million doses; he made the same amount himself in just a short amount of time, and in so doing proved that LSD was ideal for a mass movement. That many magic mushrooms couldn't possibly have grown quickly enough to meet the needs of the hundreds of thousands who took to the streets in the late sixties in opposition to the Vietnam War or went to happenings and consumed psychedelic substances as a way of rejecting the American mainstream. Neither could synthetic psilocybin, which is about one hundred times less potent than LSD, or mescaline, with its stronger side effects and more complex production method, ever have played the role that LSD now took on. Stanley gave away half of his product for free—it seemed to him that the money he made with LSD didn't really belong to him—and so the price remained low, about a dollar a trip. As for the problem of distribution, the Bear, Stanley's nickname in psychedelic circles, figured out a congenial solution. In order to reach his audience, he used the Grateful Dead, becoming the band's sound engineer. Soon the popular rock band's concerts turned into LSD happenings. Thus it wasn't Stoll's "factory" that had a hand in the mass distribution of the drug, but rather an artist named the Bear who remained in obscurity.

28

ELVIS MEETS NIXON

THE BLOODIER THE WAR IN VIETNAM BECAME, AND THE fiercer the reaction against it at home grew, the more government repression intensified. The prisons started filling up. Timothy Leary was sentenced to thirty years (!) in prison for the possession of a small amount of cannabis that border control officers found in his wife's underwear. People were locked up in maximum security prisons for LSD as well. Albert Hofmann in Switzerland began to receive a growing number of letters from American jails. His one-time wunderkind had long since turned into a problem child. To some politicians in Washington, LSD was a bigger threat to the country than the war in Vietnam. The president added his voice to those stoking panic: "These powders and pills threaten our Nation's health, vitality, and self-respect," Lyndon B. Johnson announced in a special message to Congress delivered in February 1968. He was referring not to the psychopharmaceuticals, the antianxiety and antidepressant medications with strong side effects that were sold on a massive scale at pharmacies and drugstores, but to the psychedelic substances that had been outlawed, their consumption declared a criminal act. American society was split in two over the question of LSD.

Amidst this tumultuous backdrop, in November 1968, Richard Nixon was elected president. Over the course of his time in office he would demonstrate just how much criminal energy he harbored within him, ordering a break-in at the campaign offices of his Democratic rivals, which led to the Watergate scandal and his resignation. He summed up his conception of right and wrong in concise terms: "When the president does it, that means that it is not illegal."

When Timothy Leary announced that he would challenge the California governor Ronald Reagan in his run for reelection—with John Lennon writing "Come Together" for him to use as his campaign song—Leary, whose previous conviction had been thrown out on constitutional grounds, was once again sentenced on account of a small amount of cannabis, this time to twenty years. Now Leary actually did have to report to prison, which disqualified him from running in the election. In 1971 Nixon made the government's fight against narcotics his number one issue and, continuing the work of Harry J. Anslinger, came up with a far-reaching, internationally enforced US government program, the War on Drugs. Based on the principles "eradicate, prohibit, incarcerate," the program has used up more than one trillion tax dollars to date—and has resulted in prisons being filled to capacity, a flourishing global drug mafia, and a steady rise in unregulated drug consumption worldwide. In his retirement, John Ehrlichmann, an advisor to Nixon on domestic politics, neatly summed up the president's efforts: "The Nixon campaign in 1968, and the Nixon White House after that, had two enemies: the antiwar left and black people. You understand what I'm saying? We knew we couldn't make it illegal to be either against the war or black, but by getting the public to associate the hippies with marijuana and blacks with heroin, and then criminalizing both heavily, we could disrupt those communities. We could arrest their leaders, raid their homes, break up their meetings, and vilify them night after night on the evening news. Did we know we were lying about the drugs? Of course we did."

Nixon received support for his anti-drug campaign from no less a figure than Elvis Presley, who shortly before Christmas 1970 paid his "admire[d]" president a surprise visit. A few days earlier, from

AmericanAirlines

In Flight…
Altitude;
Location;

> Dear Mr. President:
> First I would like to introduce myself.
> I am Elvis Presley and admire you
> and Have Great Respect for your
> office. I talked to Vice President
> agnew in Palm Springs 3 weeks and
> expressed my Concern for our Country.
> The Drug Culture, The Hippie Elements,
> the SDS, Black Panthers, etc. do _not_
> consider me as their enemy or as they
> call it the Establishment. I call it america and

Shaky handwriting from psychopharmaceutical abuse:
Elvis Presley warns the president about psychedelic substances.

his first-class seat aboard an American Airlines flight, the King of
Rock and Roll had written a letter to the White House, his handwriting shaky from psychopharmaceutical intake. In it he expressed
his concern for America on account of "the drug culture, the hippie
elements, the SDS, Black Panthers, etc." He was therefore prepared
to act as an undercover drug officer, and asked to be made a "Federal

Agent at Large." To emphasize his qualifications for this position he volunteered that he had "done an in-depth study of drug abuse and Communist brainwashing techniques." On top of that he had been named "one of America's Ten Most Outstanding Young Men." In a postscript to his letter, which he marked as "private and confidential," the King hastened to assure the president: "I believe that you, Sir, were one of the Top Ten Outstanding Men of America also."

Clearly Nixon was flattered by this, because he granted Elvis's request for a meeting and invited him to come to the Oval Office. It didn't hurt that his appointments secretary was also in favor of the meeting: "If the President wants to meet with some bright young people outside of the Government," the internal White House memo concluded, "Presley might be a perfect one to start with."

In the margin next to this last sentence another of Nixon's advisors had added a handwritten comment: "You must be kidding." It's not clear from the archival record whether the comment was referring to Presley's age—at thirty-five years old, he was no longer all that young—or the word "intelligent."

The bizarre meeting began at twelve-thirty p.m. on December 21, 1970. Elvis wore amber-tinted aviator sunglasses, a crimson suit, and a dark velour jacket, with a large golden belt buckle covering up his comfortable paunch. As a gift for his host he presented the president with a Colt .45 pistol from World War II, a collector's item in a hand-carved wooden box. The King quickly got to the point and voiced his conviction that the Beatles "had been a real force for anti-American spirit." They had come "to this country, made their money, and then returned to England where they promoted an anti-American theme."

Nixon looked into the bloated face of the aging rock-and-roller and nodded. "Those who use drugs," the president said in agreement, "are also those in the vanguard of anti-American protest. Violence, drug usage, dissent, protest all seem to merge in generally the same group of people."

Elvis concurred, and "indicated to the President in a very emotional manner that he was 'on [his] side,'" as the White House's

Two pills in a pod: Elvis meets Nixon at the White House.

notes from the meeting relate. One can imagine, based on these notes, how the rest of the conversation might have gone. Elvis emphasized his desire to help restore respect for the American flag: "I'm just a poor boy from Tennessee. I've gotten a lot from my country, and now I'd like to give something back. I can go right up to a group of hippies and be accepted by them, and that could be helpful for my drug drive. Say, can I get a badge for this? I collect badges, see."

Nixon gave Elvis a thoughtful look. "I'll ask my people to look into it," he assured him. "Just make sure you don't lose your credibility."

"What do you mean by that?" asked Elvis.

In lieu of a reply, Nixon suggested that he record an anti-drug anthem. He could imagine the title being something like "Get High on Life." In advance of the meeting Nixon had been briefed on the potential of such a propaganda song, since "the average American family owns four radio sets [and] 98 percent of the young people between twelve and seventeen listen to radio." Elvis, the president suggested, could record the song that would get young people back on the right track at the Narcotic Farm in Lexington—that is, at the same institution at which primarily Black inmates had been degradingly used as guinea pigs. "Don't underestimate the influence of television, either," Nixon told Elvis. His advisors had briefed him on this point as well. "Between the time a child is born and he leaves high school, it is estimated he watches between 15,000 and 20,000 hours of television. That is more time than he spends in the classroom. This is something we can pursue."

Elvis looked at Nixon, touched. He didn't say anything about the proposed song, but "in a surprising, spontaneous gesture, put his left arm around the President and hugged him." Again he said, "I'm really a big supporter of your work."

"Make sure you keep your credibility," Nixon repeated, extricated himself from Elvis's embrace, and in parting shook his hand.

Only six and a half years later, at just forty-two years old, Elvis Presley died at Graceland, his estate in Memphis, Tennessee, while defecating on the toilet. The King was severely addicted to pills, despite two stints in rehab and one course of methadone treatment, and suffered from polypharmacy, the use of too many different medications. In the first eight months of the year he died, 1977, his doctor, who would lose his license to practice medicine after the death of his most famous patient, had prescribed him more than ten thousand doses of sedatives, amphetamines, antidepressants, and opioids such as, for example, codeine—a total of more than forty pills a day. When the autopsy was performed, more than fourteen different drugs were detected in his blood. The psychopharmaceuticals prescribed over many years had led to the severe chronic constipation that required the acutely depressed singer to strain so hard on the toilet that his abdominal aorta was fatally constricted and blood could no longer get to his heart.

All these pills were legal compounds sold by international pharmaceutical companies. During his two stints in rehab, Elvis, who had grown lethargic as he neared the end, was never treated with psychedelic substances to cure him of his pill addiction—because *these* drugs had been banned by Nixon and were part of the drug culture that Elvis wanted to do something about—and in return for his efforts lost more than just his credibility.

29

A CASE OF WINE

MEANWHILE, ON THE OTHER SIDE OF THE ATLANTIC, DR. AL-
bert Hofmann was getting ready for a well-deserved retirement—
though not a well-*remunerated* retirement, as it seemed to him. In
the fifties Stoll had canceled his share of the profits in the medicines
he had developed, which had brought in billions for the company.
Since that time Hofmann had received only his regular monthly
salary. This, moreover, was lower at Sandoz than it would have been
at the local competition in Basel, at Ciba or Roche.

In 1967 the chemist had asked one last time for an increase in salary, but his request was refused, the reason given that his "current
total level of compensation [had reached] the maximum for deputy
directors." In a written reply Hofmann referred to paragraph six
of his employment contract, which stated that upon retirement an
"honorarium taking into account successes in the area of innovation" would be granted. Because he had single-handedly developed
hydergine—a medicine used to improve peripheral and cerebral
blood flow, and thus enhance brain function, as a treatment for old
age ailments—guiding it through the patent process and all the
way to its becoming a marketable product, and because this medicine occupied the top spot on Sandoz's roster in terms of sales—and
would continue to do so well into the late 1970s—he expected a bonus. Longstanding custom dictated that employees in management
positions could expect payments in the millions. There was also

another Hofmann product, Methergine, for inducing contraction in the uterus, that was still successful and was offered in Novartis's catalog as recently as 2022.

But Hofmann was to learn that the opinion of him held by the company's leadership was anything but high. Already in the last decade of his career he had had to look on as people who he believed were less qualified than he moved up the company ladder ahead of him, while he himself remained in the lab building and was never appointed to a position in upper management. Those at the top might even have been relieved that their innovation-happy chemist was leaving and wouldn't be developing yet another consciousness-altering drug that would cause the company headaches. The general director wrote back immediately telling Hofmann that he should dispense with any requests for additional compensation: "As we have informed you, the attainment of the upper limit for deputy directors is to be regarded as absolute . . . Given your salary level, I personally am of the view that any additional claims are not justified, that, on the contrary, the company is due recognition for its very generous stance. I hope that you too can align yourself with this position and won't oblige me to refer your case to the executive committee with a formal request for denial."

Even when, almost two decades later, Hofmann, long since retired, again wrote a letter petitioning his former employer—after all that time, the matter still wouldn't let him rest—almost begging for a bonus in light of the "brilliant business concluded in 1984," he was refused. It wasn't until two years after that that the company finally relented and deigned to give the man who had helped lay the foundation for Sandoz's wealth a "voluntary one-time payment of 100,000 francs"—a modest sum by Swiss standards. The reason given for it must have seemed like an insult to Hofmann: "This is made in recognition of your extraordinary contributions during the time of your employment at Sandoz." The longtime developer of medicines also received a case of wine.

The subsequent history of the Swiss pharmaceutical company was less fortunate. In Europe Sandoz has remained in collective memory as a result of a fire that broke out on November 1, 1986, in a warehouse where around nine hundred tons of highly toxic chemicals were stored, enough to wipe out the continent's entire population. In the end central Europe managed, just barely, to avoid a catastrophe like those that occurred in Bhopal or Seveso. But the discharge into the Rhine of the water used to extinguish the fire, which had become contaminated with insecticide as a result, led to a fish die-out that extended downriver as far as the Lorelei rock, four hundred kilometers away. All the eels were wiped out, along with hundreds of thousands of grayling, zander, and pike; mallards, terns, entire populations of water fleas; and almost all freshwater snails and fly larvae. The drinking water supply of several cities along the Rhine was contaminated; waterworks were forced to close. At least thirty-four different toxins, along with organic mercury compounds deadly to humans in doses of mere milligrams, ended up in the river. All told, thirty to forty tons of toxic substances were released, causing the gravest ecological harm, with consequences for nature and the human population that are still being felt to this day. It wouldn't have taken much more for the Rhine, Europe's lifeline, to have been utterly laid to waste.

In more recent years the company, whose name is scarcely ever mentioned now since the merger with Novartis, made negative headlines again when it became known that the Sandoz-made anesthetic thiopental had been used in executions at San Quentin State Prison in California.

Today, Sandoz, which once enjoyed global prominence as a brand for its mushroom-derived trial medication Indocybin and the LSD-formula Delysid, is reduced to being an unglamorous producer of generics—medicines that contain active ingredients identical to those of a formerly patent-protected formula. In 2022 Novartis announced its plans to spin off the once renowned company and list it on the market as a separate entity. Nothing remains of the Stoll era.

30

LIGHT VADER HOFMANN

ALBERT HOFMANN'S REPUTATION, ON THE OTHER HAND, JUST kept growing. Even if he was denied the Nobel Prize in Chemistry, he was awarded several honorary doctorates. In 1979 he published the autobiographical book *LSD—mein Sorgenkind* (*LSD, My Problem Child*), in which he wrote about his most important discovery and the dramatic, winding course it had taken. In his account, which doesn't make a single mention of the CIA, the chemist blames the mass distribution of LSD for use as a party drug on the fact that the substance had ended up illegal rather than being the object of research: "The history of LSD to date amply demonstrates the catastrophic consequences of misjudging its profound effect and of mistaking this substance for a pleasure drug." For the Swiss chemist there was always something sacred about the ergot derivative, in that it offered those who took it the opportunity to have life-changing experiences that allowed them to become closer to nature and brought about an understanding of their oneness with the universe. LSD, according to Hofmann, could lead to a profound ecological understanding, a reverence for life and an increased capacity to live peacefully not only with other people, but also with other species as well. Thus to him all uses of LSD for hedonistic reasons necessarily had to remain suspect, as such consumption was irreconcilable with the deep and mystical experience that he himself associated with the drug.

In the 1970s, Hofmann's drive to find a place for his discovery in a historical context led him to collaborate with the mycological researcher Gordon Wasson and the American professor of classical studies Carl Ruck, who specialized in the role of medicinal plants in Greek mythology. Together they sought to find evidence of the use of psychoactive substances in Western cultural history. Their ethnographic line of inquiry, which inspired them to consult epics like the *Odyssey* and the *Iliad*, the chronicles of classical historians like Herodotus and Thucydides, as well as depictions on ancient vases that showed ritual objects, led them to the Eleusian mysteries of ancient Greece: secret initiation rites that were part of the state cult of Athens and took place between 1500 to 300 A.D. Every September, every citizen with any sense of their own social standing paid their offering and headed off to the temple twenty kilometers away, a five-day journey punctuated by ritual sacrifices and purification ceremonies. On the sixth day, the arrival in Eleusis, the fast began, which included a prohibition on alcohol. Then the suspense started to mount: Who would be admitted to the innermost sanctum on the seventh day? There was room in the Telesterion, where the high point of the festival would be celebrated, for around three thousand initiates. But those who proved unworthy, who hadn't prepared, hadn't adhered strictly to the dietary restrictions, were turned away. Similar to present-day Berlin, where Berghain, the most famous club in the world, serves as a site of pilgrimage for aspiring partygoers who travel from all over the world hoping *to be a part of it* but who have no guarantee of being let inside, in ancient Greece too it was possible that the Eleusian bouncer would dash the would-be initiates' hopes at the last minute. Those who were allowed to enter had to swear, under penalty of death, to keep silent about what happened within. The secret was kept for two thousand years. If the surviving accounts are to be believed, those who participated in the ritual came into contact with an existence-altering force, equivalent to a spiritual rebirth. On the evening that followed the night of nights, there was a wild dance outside on the temple grounds overlooking the Bay of Eleusis and island of Salamis across the water.

"Fortunate three times over are those among mortals who, after they have seen these rites, stride off to Hades; to them alone true life is granted there," wrote Sophocles. The historical record shows that during the rites a mysterious drink was taken from sealed baskets and passed around. Was this *kykeon* hallucinogenic? Was *that* why the ritual was so legendary and powerful? Were the three thousand initiates who all took the drink at the same time in a state of alkaloid-induced ecstasy when the fertility goddess Demeter appeared before them? Did the priests of Eleusis simply have their hands on the strongest substance in ancient Greece—was that why they could host the most beloved festival in the land, a kind of Attic Burning Man? If this was the case, *which* drugs were used? Hofmann knew that the *kykeon* contained grain, which the goddess Demeter was associated with. Did the drink also include ergot?

Hofmann and his collaborators couldn't prove their theories, but still they were bold enough to offer a new interpretation of the major classical initiation rite in a jointly authored book, *The Road to Eleusis.* As Hofmann put it in a lecture, "Mysteries played a substantial role in healing, in overcoming the rift between man and nature, one can also say: in eliminating the divide between creator and created being. The cultural-historical significance can hardly be overstated. Here the Greek individual, divided and suffering in his rational, objectivizing mind, found healing in a mythical experience of wholeness that allowed him to believe in immortality within an eternal existence."

Many were inspired by these theories. Ever more frequently, Hofmann found himself acting as the guest of honor at conferences for the study of human consciousness. He became a symbolic figure, lending strength to a whole movement. It was with a measure of sadness that Hofmann noted his popularity among a niche set that sometimes displayed a tendency toward esotericism: "Instead of visiting scientific meetings and giving lectures to professionels [*sic*] I am more and more asked to address the lay public," he wrote in a letter to Humphry Osmond, who conducted research at Princeton University.

On the occasion of his one hundredth birthday on January 11, 2006, the symposium "LSD–Problem Child and Wonder Drug" was held in his honor in Basel, heralding the arrival of fresh momentum in psychedelic research, which for so long had been marginalized by prohibition and the War on Drugs. More than fifteen hundred researchers in the field of consciousness from all over the world took part. The fact that Hofmann had reached such a biblical age and yet was still full of life and in prime condition both physically and mentally seemed the best possible advertisement for the molecule he'd discovered. Over the course of the three-day forum an "appeal regarding the support of scientific research into psychoactive substances" was sent to the governments of twenty countries. The appeal's sponsors received their first positive reply from the substance's home country: "As you are no doubt aware, Switzerland, due to the stipulations put in place by the Narcotics Act [Betäubungsmittelgesetz] (BetmG), has the unique opportunity to be almost the only country . . . to permit research into psychoactive substances like LSD," wrote Pascal Couchepin, federal councilor and former president of Switzerland, in reply.

Following this development, in 2007, the Swiss psychotherapist Peter Gasser began to offer LSD and psilocybin sessions to select patients as a part of their treatment cycle. For the first time in thirty-five years, since Nixon's ban and the United Nations' Convention on Psychotropic Substances, clinical studies could be performed with the goal of developing methods of treating depression, PTSD, addictive behavior, and anxiety, starting at universities in Basel, Zurich, Freiburg, and Geneva. A dream was coming true for him, Albert Hofmann said of this development. Also in 2007, a year before Hofmann's death at 102 years old, the influential British newspaper *The Guardian* reported that the chemist and developer of medicines had been chosen the world's top living genius.

EPILOGUE: LSD FOR MOM

CONFIRMATION THAT THE SHIFT HAD FULLY TAKEN PLACE came with a 2016 paper published by Professor Roland Griffiths of Johns Hopkins University in Baltimore. In a double-blind study he demonstrated the effectiveness of psilocybin in alleviating depression and anxiety in cancer patients. Prior to this point, if a scientist had announced that they were working with psychedelics, they would have been risking their reputation and career. Since then, however, research into substances of this sort at universities in the United States and Europe has been considered serious. Thanks to private sponsors, ever more money has become available for extensive studies. A kind of gold rush has ensued, and alongside LSD and psilocybin, now referred to as "classic psychedelics," the focus has widened to include further substances like MDMA, ketamine, ibogaine, and DMT. The search is also on for entirely new molecules, with researchers working feverishly to discover substances that don't yet exist.

Today research is barreling forward full-steam ahead in the very field in which Sandoz, refusing to take up Albert Hofmann's suggestion in the mid-fifties, had failed to advance. There is talk of a start-up boom similar to what the pharmaceutical industry and Arthur Stoll experienced a century ago. During the World Economic Forum in Davos, Switzerland, in 2022, the "House of Psychedelics" dominated headlines. Substances that were simultaneously outlawed and abused by governments during the Cold War are suddenly the next big thing. In the US, MDMA is close to being granted approval by the FDA after it was recently demonstrated that the drug helps to moderate post-traumatic stress disorder, while psilocybin is being used successfully in cases of hard-to-treat depression, and LSD in cases of anxiety.

I had heard of Professor Franz Vollenweider, who leads the Neuro-psychopharmacology and Brain Imaging Unit at the University of Zurich, where he is a professor of psychiatry and chief psychiatrist and co-director of the Center for Psychiatric Research, and on top of that is director of the Heffter Research Center for Conscious-ness Studies. One main area of focus at his institute is research into the decline of mental capabilities in old age. If anyone could tell me something about LSD's latest transformation—its development from politically charged consciousness-altering drug to promising medicine—then it was he. Vollenweider could demonstrate practical results; for decades he had been investigating, with the help of PET scanners and other technology, how psychedelic substances actually work in the human brain.

His place of work is the very same place, the University of Zurich's Psychiatric Hospital, still known as the Burghölzli, where nearly eighty years ago Arthur Stoll's son Werner performed the first LSD studies on mentally ill patients. Vollenweider also gives his patients psychedelic substances; he, however, does so on a voluntary basis.

A colleague of his met me at the entrance and led me to Ward J, former home to the "Department for Unruly Women," she informed me. There was never a "Department for Unruly Men," she added incidentally before opening the door to the therapy room, which was furnished with chairs and a low table, a picture of an alpine panorama on the wall. Broad-leaved trees grew outside the window, part of a park that extended up to the border of a wood—an unspec-tacular, comfortable room, similar perhaps to the "trip chamber" at Sandoz in the mid-forties.

The sixty-eight-year-old Vollenweider radiated calm as he sat down to join me and offered me some coffee. His facial features reminded me alternately of a turtle and a bird of prey, though it was unclear which of these animals was the dominant one. He had been able to begin clinical studies of psychedelic substances as far back as 1992, since Switzerland at that time had not yet ratified the United Nations' "Convention on Psychotropic Substances." A few years into his research Vollenweider demonstrated that the classic psychedelics take effect via the 5HT2A receptors, the points of contact in the brain mentioned in the white paper I'd read when first starting my research. "The receptors are like keyholes located in the nerve cells, which the substances fit into like keys," he explained. If an LSD or psilocybin molecule is placed in one of these openings, the cell is unlocked: "It leads to a cascade of intracellular reactions. Communication between the neurons is stimulated, new connections form. Such a process is also called *learning*. In this way our memory changes, the neural network is altered and the brain's ability to react to outside influences is, in the best-case scenario, optimized. Neuroplasticity it's called, a kind of restructuring. Functional networks in the brain come into contact in a *different* fashion than they do while in a normal state and lead to altered cognition and perception. The latest studies in San Francisco suggest that stimulation of the receptors could even cause *new* neurons, i.e., new brain cells, to form. If this is borne out, it would of course be amazing."

I tried to understand what he had just told me and asked helplessly, "So taking the drugs would make a person smarter?"

"What does that mean, smarter? Reorganization of neural processes leads to a reduction in undesired thought patterns. That much has been proven."

"What kind of patterns are we talking about?" I asked.

"Habits," Vollenweider replied. "Addiction, for example. When a person compulsively believes they have to do the same thing over and over again, which can lead to feelings of inferiority, in some cases even to self-abasement. Or also to neurotic anxiety, constant negative thinking, eating disorders."

"And with LSD the brain can change this?"

"Or psilocybin, or other substances like iboga or DMT, for example. People with depression suffer from heightened perception of unpleasant impressions. The neurons are wired in such a way that entanglements form that keep continually reinforcing themselves. Rumination occurs; the person keeps falling back on primarily negative memories. Things start to spiral; the person's self-esteem collapses because they think they can't do anything about it. On psilocybin the neural network in the frontal cortex is activated in such a way that more *positive* memories are called up. As a result the negative contents of the person's consciousness are put at a greater distance; they are felt to be less overwhelming. It becomes easier to process burdensome experiences."

I took another sizable sip of coffee. My head was spinning. I remembered one of the questions I'd started out with: Why couldn't you get LSD at the pharmacy? I thought of the chaotic environment in which drugs had been dealt with for decades—of Pan and the chemist who had lost his life in his lab, and of Arthur Giuliani, who in postwar Berlin had tried in vain to regulate the black market. "And when will what you've just told me about be legally available for patients to buy?"

"That's up to the lawmakers," Vollenweider replied, and went from turtle to bird of prey. "The hurdles for approval of a psychedelic medicine are high, the necessary trials difficult if not impossible to set up. Every time you want to use a psychedelic substance you have to fight a war of paperwork, and it's not certain when you start out that you'll get the authorizations. Some drugs it's actually impossible to do research on. I'd like to work on 5-MeO-DMT for example. In my view it's a substance with potential for treatment-resistant depression. But I can't point to any studies on animals, and without toxicological data I'm not allowed to give it to people."

"Why don't you conduct your own studies on animals?"

"For us here at the Burghölzli it's too cost-intensive. We can't manage it."

"But pharmaceutical companies could?"

"Sure, they'd have the resources for it. But there's often a lack of understanding there," Vollenweider replied. "Or of will. Albert Hofmann and I, we went to Novartis once. He had just turned a hundred, and I by that point had a good twenty years of neuroscience under my belt. We proposed the idea of an Albert Hofmann Fund, for psychedelic research."

"Hofmann was pushing for something like that all the way back in the fifties," I said.

"They shot it down," Vollenweider continued. *"If we give you two money it'll just disappear.* That was more or less the response. I think for image reasons they didn't want any part of it. If they'd gone along with the idea, they'd have had a big head start today."*

"How elaborate a process is involved in developing a neuroplastic medication?"

"If you start from scratch and go in with a new drug, it takes five to seven years. But it could go faster. For the Covid vaccines for example the regulations were loosened. These are political decisions."

"How expensive is this kind of process?"

"The standard is three test phases. If you get the authorizations for working with psychedelic substances, you could make it into phase two with one to two million. There the trial includes about one hundred and twenty patients. You form control groups and administer the new drug along with an existing medication and a placebo. The key is phase three. There between three hundred and four hundred trial participants are involved. For a complete global study, pharmaceutical companies recommend about five hundred million euros. That can go up to a billion. But I think it could be done in a way that was significantly cheaper."

---

* Even more recently the pharmaceutical firm has opted not to profit from its significant discovery. "At the moment Novartis is not conducting research in connection with LSD" was the answer given in an email to the author from the Novartis press department on December 14, 2021.

"Where do you see the biggest potential uses for these kinds of medication?"

Vollenweider shrugged. "Improving neurotransmission in the brain, the modulation and reconditioning of synapses."

Then I told him about my mother and her Alzheimer's disease. "I can very much understand where you're coming from," Vollenweider said after thinking for a moment. "And that you want to do something. I myself have sometimes thought about who it is I'm actually doing the work for when I'm in the lab. One's own mother is a source of motivation."

"What do you think of microdosing?" I asked.

Again Vollenweider thought for a while. "Meaningful studies on its efficacy aren't yet available," he eventually answered. "There are, however, indications that imperceptible doses of LSD influence the functional connections between the amygdala and other key regions within the limbic system. This would suggest that the reorganization of networks regulated by the 5HT2A receptors is possible even without profound alterations in perception, as occurs with higher doses. I could imagine, however—like I said, a gut feeling, since the data aren't there—that a few high-dose applications would make more sense than a continual low dose. In general I would say that every chronically administered medication can lead to problems in the long term, through the buildup of tolerance, for example. For that reason it could be good to proceed in phases, with long-ish pauses in between—or to alternate medicines every now and then to avoid habit forming. Have you heard of hydergine? That's another one of Albert Hofmann's. Maybe worth recommending. That's available at the pharmacy, for improving blood flow in the brain. Gingko-based formulas are also interesting."

The Pandemic of Dementia

By the year 2050 the number of cases of dementia will have tripled to more than 170 million. That will mean one out of every fifty people in the world. Currently it is 57 million women and men; more than half of them suffer from Alzheimer's. And it's not only the patients themselves who are affected by the pandemic. The malicious disease changes families and puts friend networks under extreme strain, to say nothing of the burden on health systems. Countless tragedies play out in homes all over America, Asia, Africa, Europe, everywhere. The suffering is immeasurable; even today the annual global costs of Alzheimer's disease run up to a trillion dollars.

It wasn't easy to make contact with a scientist specializing in Alzheimer's. I had reached out to the Deutsches Zentrum für Neuro-degenerative Erkrankungen (DZNE)—German Center for Neuro-degenerative Diseases—a research institution that "dedicates its efforts toward all aspects of neurogenerative diseases." There are ten locations throughout Germany; the main office is in Bonn. My request to speak with someone about LSD and Alzheimer's elicited no response. Only when I followed up did the communications department offer to set up a "background conversation (without attribution by name)." On the "specific topic of LSD," however, there were "unfortunately no experts." This surprised me, since it seemed to run counter to the DZNE's claim, posted on its website, that it was working "to find novel approaches for effective prevention, therapy, and patient care."

"You know, this field is incredibly susceptible to charlatanism," the professor whom I was ultimately put in touch with said to start off the conversation. "If you go out there and say that something has this huge effect, you'll have people beating your door down. They grasp at every straw. There are so many drugs being studied at the moment, a hundred at least. You have to understand that most of them I can't say anything about. But I did read the white paper you sent me. I'll be perfectly honest: I wouldn't have expected that this was on such firm footing. These people are about to put together a more sizable trial, and if it works out as they've described it, it's an interesting approach."

"How much longer do you think it will be," I asked him, "before an effective medicine for dementia is approved?"

There was silence on the other end of the line. Had we been disconnected? Then the voice of the researcher resurfaced. "I doubt that we'll have our hands on a miracle drug within the next twenty years."

"Twenty years?" I asked, staggered. "That long?"

"The processes in the brain are multifactorial," he replied. "Pull a lever in one part and everything starts functioning properly again—unfortunately it doesn't work like that. The key word is *disease-modifying*. We need something that doesn't just alleviate symptoms, but also gets at the causes. It could take a while before we find it."

LSD Under the Christmas Tree

It was gray and cold in Zweibrücken, a small town on the far edge of the Western Palatinate where I was born and raised, and where my parents still live. In March 1945 the former ducal seat with its distinct rococo architecture had been completely destroyed in a bombing raid. Upon my arrival the sky hung low over the equally low buildings, built on the cheap after the war. It all seemed as if it were waiting for something, a bright ray of sunshine, maybe. The only light for miles around shone from the large plastic stars that hung bright and yellow over the streets.

In front of my mother was a box of medicine with "Memantine" printed on it, next to it an empty blister pack that was charred because she had stuck it in the toaster. "Oh there's no telling where this came from," she said, and fiddled with the blister pack. "These are for sick people. I'm not taking them." With these words she stood up to go lie down and sleep, her favorite activity these days. My father came and sat with me, set down two glasses and poured us both a dram of Tullamore Dew, his favorite whiskey, for the "blue hour," as my parents had always called the time of day right before sundown. "Today is bathing day," he said. "I'm already dreading it. She fights it tooth and nail when I try to get her in the shower. But she hasn't done it on her own for about a year now."

"Have you read the study?" I asked him.

"The one about this LSD?" my father replied. In his career as a judge he had risen as far as vice president of the Higher Regional Court of the Palatinate. A *man of the law*. Not a drugs guy.

"There's no guarantee that it'll work," I said. "But so far no side effects have been recorded in connection with microdosing. The amounts are so small that there's no hallucinogenic effect, no trip. But the brain is stimulated, the same receptors that are afflicted by Alzheimer's. Or at least that's what it says in the white paper."

"Yeah, yeah," he said skeptically.

"Could you imagine giving Mom one of these small doses every day? It would be a tasteless, colorless drop—it could go in a cup of coffee, for example."

"I'm supposed to give her something illegal based on *one* study?"

"It's not just one," I pushed back. "Professor Vollenweider has gotten similar results in Zurich. Research is being done all over the world, expectations are high."

"It seems strange to me," said my father. "You're not trying to tell me that they haven't looked into every single aspect of this? Wouldn't they have, if it's supposed to be promising? I mean, there could be billions in it."

"Science was hamstrung in the late sixties," I said, "when the global ban was put in place." I thought of Harry J. Anslinger and his man in Berlin, Arthur Giuliani, and decided to tell my father about my research if there was time later.

He took a sip of his whiskey. Then he closed his gray-blue eyes and said, to my surprise, "Oh, what do we have to lose?"

"You'll give it a try?"

"But now let's just assume we come to find out that it might be doing her good, this LSD . . . where would you get the stuff?"

"Let me worry about that," I said. "I've already taken care of it."

"My son," he said, giving me a searching look, "are you talking about the black market?"

•   •   •

On Christmas Eve morning the three grandkids trimmed the tree while my mother sat on the couch and flipped through photo albums. My father had put a whole stack in front of her in the hopes of stimulating her memory. Many of the old photos show my mother at parties, sitting on the end of a couch, for example, long legs crossed, one over the other, wearing a short skirt and a wide grin and flanked by laughing girlfriends. On the table in front of her are cognac glasses and a bottle of beer. The last notes of "Always on My Mind" by Elvis Presley drifted over from the record player in the living room, then a singer I didn't know began to sing "I'm So Lonesome I Could Cry." My mother turned her head and looked straight at me. "Oh, we had a good time. Why are you so sad?"

My father came from his study and sat with us.

"Because the music is so sad," I said helplessly.

"Oh come on, this is Hank Williams!" said my father. "He's not sad, he's just got soul. The first global superstar, even before Elvis. Back around the time of the Korean War. Everywhere the Yanks turned up, they had Hank Williams in tow. I've been playing him a lot lately, since I figure it might be good for the memory." He glanced over at my mother as he started telling me about the Canadian Forces Network, the radio station that they had often listened to together. Up until the late sixties, Canadian troops had been stationed in Zweibrücken, side by side with the Americans, who stayed into the nineties and had a strong influence on the life of the small town, including the nightlife. There had been, for example, the EM Club, which was reserved for enlisted members of the American armed forces—though in the late fifties my father had simply shown his German military service book, which didn't even have a photo on it, just his name and a bunch of blank pages, since he'd never served. The GI at the door always took a very close look at the booklet. Every time without fail he would flip through every single page, then smile broadly— "Welcome, comrade!"—and let my father and mother in. Inside my parents drank whiskey sours and ate their first bowl of chili. Then it was off to the always packed NCO Club, for noncommissioned officers, where they played rock and roll and on the weekends even had live country-and-western bands perform. This was at the same time that Sidney Gottlieb was running his safe houses and Arthur Giuliani and George Hunter White were secretly dosing their party guests, stamping out, little by little, the American dream.

Later it was time to open presents. Alongside the gifts for the children there was something for my mother under the Christmas tree, a blue envelope with an S on it, the Superman logo, which called to mind the old Sandoz logo. It was also my mother's first initial. Would the contents give her superpowers?

A problem now presented itself, and I remembered the scene from earlier, when my mother had eyed the Memantine prescribed by the family doctor skeptically, saying who knew where it came from, that it was for sick people and therefore not for her. I thought of the Nuremberg Code that Leo Alexander had come up with, the ethical guidelines that said that people involved in a medical experiment must understand the full extent of what the experiment entails. How were my father and I supposed to handle this? "The duty and responsibility for ascertaining the quality of the consent rests upon each individual who initiates, directs, or engages in the experiment," the code states. "It is a personal duty and responsibility which may not be delegated to another with impunity." Could we take matters into our own hands when it came to medicating my mother? The answer was obvious: We had to ask her. Thankfully this was possible, despite her illness. She *was* able to make decisions; she was constantly speaking up in favor of or against something.

The next morning, Christmas Day, it was raining so heavily that we had to put off our planned visit to the cemetery where my grandparents were buried. The drip coffee at breakfast had perked me up, given me confidence. I sat down next to my mother on the sofa in the living room, removed the little plastic bottle from the blue envelope and placed it on the coffee table among the magazines and a bowl full of Christmas cookies. "I brought this for you," I said. "LSD."

"Oh, that's for me?" my mother replied, and laughed. "So I'm getting really weird stuff now, is that it?"

"Some people call it a *drug*," I said. "But there are scientists, they've found out that it's a promising medicine." I looked at her. "Do you feel like giving it a try?"

"If you say so, son of mine!" she answered, and picked up the little bottle, turning it around in her hand and looking at it.

"I'd also take a drop," I said. "It comes from Switzerland."

"Oh, from Switzerland." My mother patted my thigh with her hand. "Oh, honey. I'm so glad."

"So that's a yes?"

"Well, go on, do it already," my mother replied. "Don't talk so much all the time. Do it!"

I told my father about this conversation, and together we decided to try it, based on the scientific evidence that was available thus far of the positive effects of microdoses of LSD for Alzheimer's disease. Following her midday nap and before our afternoon walk my mother, my father, my sister, her husband, and I each took a drop of lysergic acid diethylamide: 12.5 micrograms dissolved in coffee, a vanishingly small dose.

We walked along the creek and past the public pool. The sky was gray, but in the west the clouds were starting to clear, and maybe a little sunshine would come through after all. My brother-in-law asked me if the current research still worked under the premise that, as Aldous Huxley described it, psychedelics opened the "doors of perception." I remembered what Franz Vollenweider had told me about this: Sensory impressions arrive first in the thalamus, located in the diencephalon or interbrain. There they are rerouted and sent on their way to the cerebral cortex. His brain scans had shown that under the influence of LSD and psilocybin *more* sensory impressions are allowed through from the thalamus. So it was as Huxley had determined in his self-experiments, when he spoke of experiencing a flood of perceptions where before there was just a trickle. This surplus bounty of images, sounds, and smells was processed by the gray matter in the cerebral cortex, the frontal cortex, to a *lesser* extent than it would be in a state of sobriety. Sensory impressions were thus evaluated less. "You perceive a greater quantity of things, but do less classifying of them," I said to my brother-in-law.

"Less research, more *being*," said my sister, grinning, teasing me.

"They've also determined that the decision center in the brain receives *less* energy on LSD, so that peripheral regions of the brain can become more active. So for example you see this tree here." I pointed at a beech on the riverbank. "Without your being conscious of it happening, your ego tells you: That's a tree, it looks pretty, is good for the climate, poses no danger, and so we like and enjoy it. The ego puts the world in order, categorizes it. But when the ego is supplied with less energy and takes a step back, and peripheral regions of the brain get to simply perceive the tree, not immediately sticking it into any kind of conceptual framework but instead just letting it be *in and of itself*, then that's something else. There's suddenly less separation between us and the tree, and this is perceived as an exhilarating feeling of *oneness*."

"Rarely have I enjoyed a gray day as much as I have this one," my sister commented with a smile.

My mother walked on ahead of us, holding the dog on a leash.

"I don't feel a thing," said my father. "I think they sold you water."

I walked a little faster to get ahead and let my mother hook her arm through mine. She was in good spirits, was probably happy that the family was all there together. All of a sudden she started singing: "Now we're going dancing together, I'm healthy, you're healthy . . ." Her right hand, which was holding the leash, bounced up and down in the air, conducting. "Come on, you dance too!" she cheerily commanded me. "Oh God, my dear, come here, you're so sweet." She leaned toward me and gave me a kiss on the forehead. "That's the woods up ahead, when we get there we'll turn around and go straight back home. You do have a girlfriend, don't you? Oh, tell her she should come! It's no problem. She can stay with us anytime. You know that!"

"Yes," I said.

"It's not bad, everything's nice and easy, nice and easy," said my mother. She slid her arm out from mine and ran her hand through my hair. When we reached the edge of the Palatinate Forest we turned around and went back. Just as she had suggested.

That evening she showered on her own, voluntarily, for the first time in twelve months.

Drop Days

Over the following weeks my mother took LSD at irregular intervals, with long-ish pauses in between. These "drop days" differed from those without the substance, my father told me. My mother was downright ebullient; instead of dutifully taking her midday nap she sat bolt upright in bed, tapping out rhythms on the duvet. Sometimes she sang or talked nonstop, in long sentences that she could no longer form without lysergic acid diethylamide. In the nights that followed she talked in her sleep more frequently than usual, saying things of a complexity that surprised my father and kept him up. Albert Hofmann had once been looking for a stimulant drug: He had found it in LSD, which also boosts the release of dopamine. The drops massaged my mother's brain, brought color to her cheeks; her occasional oppressive lethargy and apathy were swept away. On LSD my mother was more lively, harder to keep in check—harder to control. The daily routine broke down somewhat, that rhythm my father needed to take care of the thousand things that my mother's care demanded of him every day—that habitual sequence of things that did her good as well.

But he kept at it, because for the first time he felt like he had his hands on something that might possibly make a difference in the face of this severe personality-altering illness.

Five months later, on Mother's Day, I was back in Zweibrücken for another visit. At tea my mother reached for the local paper, smoothed the page with her fingers, and squinted; clearly she was concentrating. "Ma-s-sive arms aid for . . . ," she read aloud. Then she stopped, stuck on a word she didn't know. "U-kr-a-in-e."

"Man, look at that, you're reading again!" My father gazed at her in amazement. "In the past year you haven't even looked at a newspaper, much less picked one up and started reading from it!"

Now he looked over at me. Yes, it was working.

House of Psychedelics

On March 11, 1963, Albert Hofmann wrote to Aldous Huxley: "In our Western civilization the Tabu [*sic*] is missing which regulates the [use of] psychedelic drugs by primitive people. It is difficult to replace Tabu by government regulations and therefore it is of paramount importance to know what kind of person and organizations are de[a]ling with the application and distribution of psychedelic drugs."

Priests like the ones in ancient Greece or shamanic healers like those in the Mexican mountain village of Huautla do not play a role in our society. For now there are people like Pan who can help out every now and then at the Zurich train station, but this is against the law and can't be the solution. It's true that the end of the prohibition of psychedelics is next in line after the legalization of cannabis, but a legal process is not sufficient. We must develop a new approach to substances that have an effect on our consciousness and primarily represent not a danger but an opportunity. A discourse must develop concerning the approval of psychedelic medicines and the promotion of research. The ban on molecules that broaden our perception seems anachronistic, like a kind of biochemical wall that the government puts up inside people's heads: thus far and no further. In so doing, the democratic countries of the West especially, whose appeal and whose prosperity are based on the freedom of the individual, do themselves a disservice.

Like Arthur Giuliani in postwar Berlin, walking through a world of ruins and trying to establish order in an effort to make life more worth living, we too are now standing before a giant ash heap, one that the "War on Drugs" has left in its wake. But unlike the narcotics control officer Giuliani, his boss Anslinger, President Nixon, and all the governments of the world that followed their example, we should refrain from making the mess any bigger—should let scientific findings guide us in how we move forward, not the ideologies of yesterday. The time for a turnaround is now.

ACKNOWLEDGMENTS

My thanks to my agents Andrew Nurnberg in London and Robin Straus in New York, as well as to my former publisher Helge Malchow, who lent his practiced eye to editing the book. I thank Marshall Yarbrough, representing all my translators, who drove me five hours through heavy snow to the Penn State University Archive, where the Anslinger papers are kept—and five hours back. That's dedication! I'd also like to thank Olivier Mannoni for the French translation. Our close collaboration was an inspiration to me!

This book would not have been possible without the assistance of archivists. My sincere thanks to Florence Wicker and Walter Dettwiler at the Novartis archive. Also of great help were Thomas Notthoff and Florian Spillert at the archive of the Max Planck Society in Berlin, as well as Stefan Hächler, head of the archive of the Institut für Medizingeschichte at the University of Bern and the man in charge of the Albert Hofmann Papers. Recognition is due to Ken Dornstein and Amir Bar-Lev, two filmmakers who shared their information with me. The spirit of sharing also lives in Egmont R. Koch, who made his research on Beecher and what went on at Harvard available to me. Thank you also to Sarah Elmer, my die-hard test reader.

In Switzerland I received support from the team at the ALPS conference in Lausanne and from the psychotherapist Peter Gasser, as well as from Andreas Hofmann, Albert Hofmann's son. My thanks to Beat Bächi, who showed me such wonderful hospitality on the Oberänzi. I will also mention Günter Engel, former chemist at Sandoz and colleague of Albert Hofmann. It was he who provided the hand-drawn diagram of the LSD molecule that appears in this book. Equally helpful was Tim Schlidt, who sent me the white paper, the team at the Horizons Conference, and Jitka Nikodemova, who helped me with research. Manfred Kopp, historian in Oberursel, also deserves mention; likewise Ilona Fehr, who helped me to coordinate the meeting with Franz Vollenweider. Special thanks are due to Professor Vollenweider himself for the valuable information and his inspiring character. The same goes for Leonard Pickard, who made many things clear to me over the course of many long conversations, and for Douglas Gordon, for the enigmatic picture on the German cover.

I am certain to have forgotten someone in this list, and for that I am sorry. Clearly it is unavoidable for things to go missing in the void of that black box that is our head. In any case I will mention my children—quite simply because one has one's children to thank for everything. The same goes for my parents, especially in this case. From my heart I thank you, dear Dad, for your generosity, your help, and your love. And I would like to thank my mother, for all the affection she has already given me and still continues to give me. I owe everything to my upbringing in my parents' home in Zweibrücken.

Berlin, 2023

NOTES

1. The Zone

4 Washington Daily News *reported:* Curt Reiss, "Berlin Black Market Booming, Sky Is Limit on Watches, Dope," *Washington Daily News*, 24 July 1945.

4 *"the history of western civilisation":* Jähner, *Aftermath*, 180.

4 *"form of law violation":* Arthur Giuliani to Branch Chief, Office of Military Government for Germany (US), Internal Affairs and Communications Division, Public Safety Branch, APO 742, 23 September 1946, "Narcotic Law Enforcement by German Police Agencies," NARA, NND 978040.

5 *and put into circulation:* LAB/B 36/4/23–2/18, Report of Narcotic Control Situation, Berlin District, 3 June 1946, 1; depiction of the "Office of Military Government Berlin Sector" from 8 August 1947, 3.

5 *pills of cocaine, 0.003 grams:* "Submitted as an annex to a letter to the League of the Red Cross Societies in Geneva, Switzerland, forwarded to the Bureau of Narcotics on July 25, 1945, by the Civil Affairs Division of the War Department," NARA, NND 978040; LAB/B 36/4/23–2/18, Report of Narcotic Control Situation, Berlin District, 3 June 1946, 5.

5 *"by the Nazi underground":* Memorandum of conversation, "Narcotic Control in Germany," 24 July 1945, NARA, NND 978040.

5 *be wrong with that:* Harry J. Anslinger, the son of German-Swiss immigrant parents, had taken office as commissioner of the Federal Bureau of Narcotics in 1930 to oversee the country-wide ban on alcohol during Prohibition. In being nominated to this position he had gotten help from his wife's uncle, the immensely wealthy Andrew C. Mellon, finance

minister under President Hoover and owner of the sixth-largest bank
in America, the Mellon Bank. The family also owned the Old Over-
holt Whiskey Distillery, the oldest distillery in the US, for which
reason Anslinger made sure that it received authorization allowing
it to continue selling its high-proof product during the Prohibition
years "for medicinal purposes"—medicinal whiskey. Anslinger's attempt to keep Americans from drinking was a fiasco. Alcohol didn't
go away, but the mob became entrenched, raking in a fortune from
illegal booze, and with the mob came corruption. Anslinger had to
fire a third of his agents for taking bribes, and the alcohol ban's re-
peal in 1933, three years after he took office, seemed like capitulation.
His resources were cut, the fleet of cars at his disposal so radically
reduced that gangsters like Al Capone, who had made it big thanks
to Prohibition, left him in the dust: "They use fast cars—Lincolns or
Cadillac cars," he complained at a hearing before Congress (McWilliams, *The Protectors*, 64). Every year the budget was cut by another
10 percent, and the FBN was at risk of becoming insignificant. But
Anslinger didn't give up. He decided to create a new enemy, one that,
unlike alcohol, didn't have a lobby in Washington. To that end he set
his sights on a plant that up until then no one had seen any harm in,
cannabis, used for hundreds of years and available in large quantities both in the United States and in neighboring Mexico. Anslinger
was supported in his crusade by William Randolph Hearst, head of
what at the time was the largest media empire in the world, with over
twenty-five daily newspapers and weeklies, a dozen radio stations,
two news agencies, a film studio, and one of the first television stations ever. Again and again his news organs reported on Mexicans
that came over the border illegally in order to defile white women
while intoxicated on cannabis. From that point forward Anslinger no
longer called cannabis by its common English name but rather engi-
neered this reassessment of the medicinal plant turned devil's weed
on a linguistic level as well, using the Spanish term "marijuana" because it sounded foreign and Mexican, so therefore threatening.

6   *"brief summer of anarchy"*: Jähner, 186.
6   *"not yet in sight"*: Giuliani to Anslinger, date unknown, NARA, NND
    978040.
7   *"years of the war"*: Letter from Mittelhaus quoted in Anslinger to
    Giuliani, 8 October 1946; the following two quotes as well. NARA,
    NND 978040. Cf. Holzer, *Die Geburt der Drogenpolitik*, 314.
7   *"material for our organization"*: Anslinger to Giuliani, 8 October 1946,
    NARA, NND 978040.

7   *"entirely satisfactory"*: "Submitted as an annex . . . ," NARA, NND 978040; the following two quotes as well.

7   *"in pre-war Germany"*: Giuliani to Branch Chief, 23 September 1946, NND 978040.

7   *territories during the war:* Memorandum of conversation, "Narcotic Control in Germany," 24 July 1945, NARA, NND 978040. Cf. Collins, *Legalising the Drug Wars,* 93.

7   *"severity as in the past"*: "Submitted as an annex . . . ," NARA, NND 9788040.

8   *FBN district supervisors:* McWilliams, 84. The matter landed on the desk of President Roosevelt, who on the advice of the pharmaceutical lobby decided against firing his top drug enforcer.

8   *"good as white men"*: Newton, *Marijuana,* 183.

8   *"when he is cleared"*: Giuliani to Anslinger, 17 October 1946, NARA, NND 978040; the following three quotes as well.

9   *policemen in active service:* Giuliani to Anslinger, 27 October 1946, NARA, NND 978040; the following three quotes as well.

9   *"central control authority"*: Samuel Breidenbach to the Chief, Public Health Branch, G-5 United States Forces, European Theater, 22 September 1945, NARA, NND 978040, 0660, Folder 1; the following three quotes as well.

9   *"not stop before frontiers"*: "Submitted as an annex . . . ," NARA, NND 978040.

9   *"might have its origin"*: Breidenbach to the Chief, Public Health Branch, G-5 United States Forces, European Theater, 22 September 1945, NARA NND 978040, 0660, Folder 1.

10 *"Allied Control Authority"*: Giuliani to Anslinger, date unknown, NARA, NND 978040.

10 *newly founded United Nations:* Cf. Holzer, 296: "The efficient management of drug control in occupied Germany was instrumental to underscoring the legitimacy of America's claim to a leading role on drug policy in the eyes of the international community."

10 *consistent with his worldview:* Ibid., 295.

12 *"the face of ignorance"*: Giuliani to Anslinger, 7 November 1946, NARA, NND 978040.

12 *"part of the Soviets"*: Giuliani to Anslinger, 24 December 1946, NARA, NND 978040.

12 *"line with stupefying monotony"*: Ibid.

12 *"do business with" him:* Giuliani to Anslinger, 3 December 1946, NARA, NND 978040; also the following quote. Cf. Giuliani to Anslinger, 15 January 1947.

12 *"rough on the nerves"*: Giuliani to Anslinger, 3 December 1946, 14 November 1946, and 24 December 1946, NARA, NND 978040.

12 *"achieve uniformity of application"*: Giuliani to Anslinger, 15 January 1947, NARA, NND 978040.

13 *"be described as egotistics"*: Giuliani to Anslinger, 14 November 1946, NARA, NND 978040.

13 *"just about a washout"*: Anslinger to Giuliani, 18 April 1947, NARA, NND 978040.

13 *"far outpaced Giuliani's assessment"*: Statement by Harry J. Anslinger in Lake Success, New York, 9 December 1946, Barch-Koblenz/Z 45 F/5/329–1/10.

13 *"I have ever had"*: Giuliani to Anslinger, 24 December 1946. NARA, NND 978040.

2. From Paint to Medicine

15 *"transforming psychedelics into medicines"*: Eleusis company website, https://www.eleusisltd.com.

15 *"disease modifying therapeutic" for Alzheimer's*: Raz, "Lysergic Acid Diethylamide," 1.

16 man with *"community spirit"*: Andreas Hofmann, conversation with author, 11 November 2021, Basel, Switzerland; Frank Petersen (head of natural substances research at Novartis), conversation with author, 24 March 2022, Novartis Campus, Basel, Switzerland; Brüschweiler, Diggelmann, and Lüthy, *Sammlung Arthur Stoll*, 1961, ix and x.

17 *a unique, daunting task:* Willstätter seemed not to take it amiss when Stoll left his research lab for the job at Sandoz. "I write you today to once more sincerely wish you luck with the new life path that you have chosen, with your position, your work, and your new home, and to once again extend my heartfelt thanks for all your work in these rich and scientifically fruitful years" (Willstätter to Stoll, 11 September 1917, ETH: Hs 1426a:71).

17 *he later described:* Arthur Stoll, "35 Jahre Mutterkornforschung und industrielle Mutterkornverwertung, Referat in der Sitzung vom 5.3.1953 des Verwaltungsrates der Sandoz AG Basel," Novartis Company Archive: C 102.001 (1953–54), 1.

17 *"imitating the competition's medicines"*: Ibid.

18 *Stoll described it:* Ibid., 2.

19 *lower Rhine in 857:* Bauer, *Das Antonius-Feuer in Kunst*, cited in Schmersahl, "Mutterkorn," 48. The earliest proof of the toxicity of ergot came

from experiments on animals conducted by Denis Dodart, one of the
personal physicians to Louis XIV.

20 *was becoming too protracted:* Stoll, "35 Jahre Mutterkornforschung," 2–3.

20 *"drive doctors to despair":* Ibid.

20 *"the one before him":* Ibid.

21 *"impact of this discovery":* Ibid., 1, 6.

21 *director of the company:* Meanwhile, Stoll never forgot what he owed his
mentor: "There was scarcely a scientific discussion with Professor Stoll
in which he failed to mention his revered teacher Professor Willstätter
and his work in Willstätter's laboratory," confirmed Albert Hofmann,
the discoverer of LSD, whom Stoll hired in 1929 as a chemist at Sandoz
(Hofmann, *LSD, My Problem Child,* 21). For Hofmann the fact that
Sandoz's lab worked with natural materials was a crucial factor in his
decision to work at the company, even though he had had other options.

4. On Location: Novartis Company Archive

25 *"the chemical-pharmaceutical industry":* Wirtschaftsarchivportal, Novartis archive page, http://www.wirtschaftsarchivportal.de/archiv/details
/id/94.

5. The Mice Don't Notice a Thing

30 *"are welcome to try":* Hofmann, *LSD, My Problem Child,* 10.

30 *"ergotamine for your experiments":* Ibid., 13.

32 *Arthur Stoll recalled:* Arthur Stoll, "35 Jahre Mutterkornforschung
und industrielle Mutterkornverwertung, Referat in der Sitzung vom
5.3.1953 des Verwaltungsrates der Sandoz AG Basel," Novartis Company Archive: C 102.001 (1953–54), 6.

32 *"research program for good":* Moser, "Psychotropes Wissen–Figuren," 101.

32 *"on me without cease":* Albert Hofmann, log book entry, 19 April 1943,
vol. 2, Novartis Company Archive, H-203.005; Albert Hofmann, log
book entry, 16 April 1943, Novartis Company Archive, H-105.022. Cf.
Albert Hofmann, "Wie das Phantasticum LSD 25 entdeckt wurde," 7
December 1952, 1.

33 *"was just really stubborn":* Günter Engel, conversation with author, 5
November 2021, Weil am Rhein, Germany.

33 *"still to be expected":* Hofmann, log book entry, 19 April 1943, and
Hofmann, log book entry, 16 April 1943. Cf. Hofmann, "Wie das Fantas-
ticum," 1. The following quotes here as well.

34 *"took on uncanny dimensions"*: Hofmann, "Betr. D-Lysergsäure-diäthylamid, Bericht über einen Selbstversuch mit einer toxischen Dosis d-Lysergsäure-diäthylamid-tartrat," 22 April 1943, Novartis Company Archive, H-105.022. The following two quotes as well.

35 *"deep, blood pressure normal"*: Walter Schilling, "Beobachtungen bei Dr. A. Hofmann nach Einnahme von 0.25 mg des Diaethylamids der Lysergsäure am 19.4.43," Hofmann Papers, 148.1.f, 1.

35 *"image, shifting kaleidoscope-like"*: Hofmann, "Betr. D-Lysergsäure-diäthylamid," 4.

35 *strongest stuff in the world*: Ibid.; the following quote as well.

35 *"could have an effect"*: "Stanislav Grof Interviews Dr. Albert Hofmann," 25.

36 *up for the war*: Hofmann, "Betr. D-Lysergsäure-diäthylamid," 4.

36 *played "footballino and billiards"*: Albert Hofmann, "Bericht über 3 Selbstversuche mit d-Lysergsäure-diäthylamid," 30 December 1943, Hofmann Papers, 148.1.3; the two following quotes as well.

37 *new substances, would note*: Ibid., as well as Albert Hofmann to Arthur Stoll, 27 October 1944.

7. Agrochemistry

42 *"old fields before sundown"*: Cf. Bächi, *LSD auf dem Land*, 21.

42 *the Emmental put it*: Dr. Carl Meyer to Prof. Dr. Stoll, 21 February 1941, Novartis Company Archive: Sandoz, H-202.024.

42 *shortfalls in grain production*: Novartis Company Archive: Sandoz, H-202.019.

43 *the price of rye*: "Detaillierte Statistiken zu Ernte, Abnahme etc. 1955," Novartis Company Archive: Sandoz H-202.003. Cited in Bächi, 73.

43 *a "reliable mass infection"*: Bächi, 65.

44 *thirty-one inoculation machines*: Ibid.

44 *specially engaged "machine managers"*: Ibid.

46 *Novartis International AG*: Novartis Company Archive, email to author, 10 November 2021.

47 *side of the Allies*: Independent Commission of Experts Switzerland, *Switzerland, National Socialism*, 22.

48 *"integration without political participation"*: Ibid., 23–24, and Thomas Maissen, "Weshalb blieb die Schweiz im Zweiten Weltkrieg verschont?" *Neue Zürcher Zeitung*, 8 August 2018.

8. LSD in the Archive

50   *"world of the mind"*: Aldous Huxley to Albert Hofmann, 3 August 1958, Hofmann Papers, Box 136.

9. Arthur Stoll's Art

54   *maintained in "strict confidence"*: Arthur Stoll, letter, 7 December 1931, Max Planck Society Archive, III, Abt., Rep. 25, Bestell-Nr.: 253; the following quote as well.

55   *"for further investigation"*: Arthur Stoll, letter, 22 July 1926.

55   *and Stoll Swiss:* Richard Kuhn, letter, 19 November 1945.

56   *"boards under all circumstances"*: Fritz Augsberger to Arthur Stoll, 6 April 1933 (second letter), https://www.dodis.ch/temporary-cache /public/pdf/18000/dodis-18559-uek.pdf. Cf. SAR, M-320.10., 169, n. 2.

56   *executive than commercial interests:* Independent Commission of Experts Switzerland, 328: "It was only too clear that the firm's immediate accommodation was based purely on commercial interests and that humanitarian considerations and the political implications of the company's personnel policy were not of great importance." Accordingly, every letter to Stoll from Nuremberg from that point on ended with "mit deutschem Gruß," i.e., "Heil Hitler." Cf. Augsberger to Stoll, 28 November 1938, Eidgenossische Technische Hochschule (ETH), Hs1426b:12. It's possible that Stoll simply lacked empathy: In a letter from summer 1933 he wrote to his just-fired mentor Willstätter to rave about his new "eight-cylinder Cadillac," a "wonder of automotive technology," whose "driving safety probably cannot be exceeded," emphasizing "the comfort and ease of driving, absence of noise, and beautiful interior" (Stoll to Willstätter, July 1933, ETH: Hs1426b:12).

56   *"of handicapped people"*: Independent Commission of Experts Switzerland, 304.

56   *who the suppliers were:* Ohler, *Der totale Rausch,* 36–37.

56   *Werner Mittelhaus had worked:* Holzer, 314: Ampules of morphine found use "in great quantity for killings within the framework of decentralized euthanasia measures."

56   *to the mass murderers:* Independent Commission of Experts Switzerland, 308.

57   *"your circle of acquaintances"*: Arthur Stoll to Richard Willstätter, 20 August 1935, Schweizerisches Kunstarchiv, HNA 92.1.10.

57   *Willstätter in December 1938:* Arthur Stoll to Richard Willstätter, 3 December 1938, ETH: Hs1426a:392.

57 *"was to enrich themselves"*: Willstätter, *Aus meinem Leben*, 368.

58 *"to travel abroad difficult"*: Richard Willstätter to Arthur Stoll, 11 November 1938, ETH: Hs1426a:362: "Yesterday four Gestapo people came to my home, who were led around the house by Elise, since I had just gone out to my garden."

58 *"you and our science"*: Arthur Stoll to Richard Willstätter, 1 December 1938 and 10 December 1938, ETH: Hs1426a:390.

58 *his fortune remained behind*: Willstätter, letter, 21 February 1939, ETH: Hs1426a423.

58 *"to our company first"*: ETH: Hs1426a:41.

59 *"it transferred to us"*: Ibid.

59 *former level of productivity*: Hermann Hesse, letter, January 1948, ETH: Hs1426b:300.

59 *in an embittered letter*: Arthur Stoll to Elise Schnauffer, 10 August 1944, ETH: Hs1426.

10. The Other Richard

61 *"will is our faith"*: Lothar Jaenicke, "Richard Kuhn, das Dritte Reich und die GDCh," *Nachrichten aus der Chemie, Zeitschrift der Gesellschaft Deutscher Chemiker* 5 (2006): 511. Cf. Schmaltz, *Kampfstoff-Forschung*, 380.

61 *"a threefold Sieg Heil"*: Deichmann, *Flüchten, Mitmachen*, 416.

61 *deadliest in the world*: Kuhn stated his views publicly again and again, for example in 1936, when in a letter to the general secretary of the Kaiser-Wilhelm Society he denounced his colleague Otto Fritz Meyerhof, the winner of the Nobel Prize in 1922: "An inquiry made to the State Police gives me occasion to ask you to have the questionnaires of those working at our Institute for Physiology closely examined. I have told Herr Prof. Meyerhof for his part that I do not intend to exert control over his choice of employees. This, however, applies only under the condition that in each and every case he send properly filled-out questionnaires to the general administration in Berlin. Apparently at this moment there are persons of non-Aryan origin employed at the Institute under Herr Prof. Meyerhof (Herr Lehmann, Frl. Hirsch, and another lady whom I do not yet know), a fact which invites questioning of the Kaiser Wilhelm Society as a whole and the Heidelberger Institute in particular. I would like to suggest that, after looking through the questionnaires, you give Herr Prof. Meyerhof precise guidelines to adhere to in the selection of his group of employees. In order to give unambiguous expression to the stance of the Kaiser Wilhelm Society and to head off the aforemen-

tioned questioning, it would also be of importance in view of these guidelines to make it known not only in a letter to Herr Prof. Meyerhof but also in a memorandum to all local partner institutes, even though there exist no similar cases to this one . . . Appealing to you was the only path that I saw to keep our Institute, as wonderful as it is, together. Kind regards, Heil Hitler!" In his reply, the general secretary played down the issue: "Regarding employment of persons of non-Aryan descent under Prof. Meyerhof, we know only of the cases of Lehmann and Hirsch, who, because they are not employees, but rather work in the institute as guests or as doctoral candidates, as such are not subject to registration with the general administration of the Kaiser Wilhelm Society." Max Planck Society Archive, Abt. 1, Rep. IA 540/2.

61 *"know who's behind this"*: Nasher, *Entlarvt!*, 97.

62 *"was always the same"*: Ibid.

62 *rendered the defendant submissive:* Scopolamine is an alkaloid of nightshades such as henbane, belladonna, jimsonweed, and mandrake. In high doses it is said to cause a state of submissiveness and was therefore considered as a potential truth drug.

62 *"Reich Main Security Office"*: National Archives Great Britain: KV 2/471, as well as "Operation Neapolitan": HS 1/189, 112, 117, 119, 129, 130; the previous quote as well. See also Müller, *Im Auftrag der Firma,* 258, fn. 1717.

63 *"which I received safely"*: Richard Kuhn to Arthur Stoll, 20 October 1943, Novartis Company Archive, C.201.052. The full text of the letter reads as follows:

> Herr Prof. Dr. A. Stoll
> Sandoz Chemical Factory
> Basel
>
> My Dear Herr Professor Stoll!
>   My sincerest thanks for the shipment of the 5 x 0.1 grams of ergotamine tartrate, which I received safely.
>   I would also like to take this opportunity to let you know that we had a daughter, Linde, on October 8. My wife and the little one are both well.
>   Best regards,
>   Your very devoted,
>   Richard Kuhn

11. Brainwashing

65   *"Neutralization of the Will"*: Ohler, *Der totale Rausch,* 277.

66   *"questions were cleverly put"*: "U.S. Naval Technical Mission in Europe, Technical Report no. 331–45. 'German aviation medical research at the Dachau concentration camp,' Oct. 1945," Harvard Medical Library in the Francis A. Countway Library of Medicine: H MS c64, Box 11, f. 75.

12. The Trip Chamber

69   *"sit and lie down"*: Stoll, "Lysergsäure-diäthylamid," 4.

70   *"a little-known substance"*: Ibid., 5.

70   *was reported to say:* Ibid., 19. The following quotes here as well.

70   *"alterations to mental life"*: Ibid., 12.

70   *"effectiveness justifies further trials"*: Ibid., 32.

71   *"L.S.D. incl. 2 pipettes"*: "Berichte von Sebstversuchen mit d-Lysergsäure-diäthylamidtartrat, 1943–1946": Dr. Werner Stoll, Assistant at the Burghölzli Cantonal Clinic, to Prof. Dr. med. Ernst Rothlin, head of the pharmacological laboratory at Sandoz A.G., 7 May 1945 (copy). Hofmann Papers: 148.10a.

71   *wrote Werner Stoll:* Ibid.; the following quote as well.

71   *after "three LSD trials"*: Stoll, "Lysergsäure-diäthyladmid," 28; the following quote as well.

71   *"severe endogenous emotional disorders"*: Ibid.

13. Alsos

73   *"the benefit" of America"*: Müller, *Im Auftrag der Firma,* 262.

73   *forced back the Wehrmacht:* The code name Alsos was used in reference to the unit's supreme commander, General Leslie R. Groves. This went against intelligence service usage, as the name could be too easily linked to one of the persons active in it—for which there was internal criticism. Groves also led the Manhattan Project.

74   *"American and British sway"*: Henze, "Recollections of a Medical Intelligence Officer," 970.

74   *"infectious diseases, vaccines, etc"*: Ibid., 967; the following quote as well.

75   *"we ourselves would develop"*: Ibid., 968.

75   *albeit "with some exceptions"*: Müller, 286; the following quote as well.

76   *"to the Allied forces"*: "Captain Carlo Henze," 5 April 1947, FA Novartis: M 370.010c., 1942–52.

14. The Missing Box

78 *"every nightmare come true"*: Jacobsen, *Operation Paperclip,* 121 and 123.

79 *"trustworthy" without anyone objecting*: Julien Reitzenstein, *Himmlers Forscher,* 202.

79 *"understanding and enlightened decision"*: "Trials of War Criminals before the Nuremberg Military Tribunals under Control Council Law No. 10," vol. 2, Washington, DC: US Government Printing Office (1949), 181–82.

15. Advisor Kuhn

80 *was also in attendance:* Richard Kuhn to Arthur Stoll, 10 May 1948, Novartis Company Archive: C201.052, "Korrespondenz mit Kuhn."

80 *letter marked* TOP SECRET: Albarelli, *A Terrible Mistake,* 362–63; the following three quotes as well.

81 *"DM 972 per month"*: Max Planck Society Archive, III, Abt., Rep. 25, Nr. 253, Bestell-Nr.:12. (The quotation is translated from German; it is not a verbatim rendering of the source quote. —Trans.)

81 *"scientific material, scientific consultations"*: "Genehmigung für Kuhn: Reise vom 16.8–15.948, Ausstellung eines Interzonen-Passes," Max Planck Society Archive, III, Abt., Rep. 25, Nr. 253, Bestell-Nr.:12.

81 *"The New Hallucinatory Agent"*: Albarelli, 363; the following quotes as well.

82 *Stoll wrote from Basel:* Arthur Stoll, letter, 24 August 1948, Max Planck Society Archive, III, Abt., Rep. 84/2; the following quote as well.

82 *"[his] sister-in-law"*: Kuhn, letter, 18 June 1948, FA Novartis: C 201.052. "Charitable shipments" also ensued: Stoll sent his "very devoted" friend in still ravaged Germany "10 tins of powdered whole milk, 92 lightbulbs, 46 rolls of film, 6 dozen photo plates, 2 kg photo copy paper." A memorandum written by Stoll shows how deeply the German was able to insinuate himself into the development of Sandoz compounds: "Professor Kuhn mentions that the sensitivity of certain people to chemical substances is inherited, i.e., rooted in the genes, and suggests . . . investigating the sensitivity to ergot alkaloids with regard to genetics. Such a study could indeed yield interesting results and maybe also clear up some contradictions that we are currently encountering in connection with the effect of ergot alkaloids on various persons" (Arthur Stoll, "Aktennotiz über eine Unterredung mit Hern Prof. Dr. Richard Kuhn, am Donnerstag, den 31. August 1950"). Stoll became even more explicit: "Incidentally he promised to send us all

the biological studies performed by his institute and is also prepared to receive people from our laboratory at his own and introduce them to his working methods . . . I consider it very important that we apply on ergot the major discoveries made by Prof. Kuhn's laboratory in Heidelberg in the forming of mutants of lower organisms, all the more so since Prof. Kuhn is prepared to offer us any advice or assistance we may need, including from an equipment standpoint" (Ibid.).

16. Pork Chops

84   *"German people to starve"*: Reeves, *Daring Young Men,* 6.
84   *"all means are justified"*: Kopp, "Lesen wie in einem offenen Buch," 81. (This quote has been translated from Kopp's German; it is not a verbatim rendering of the English source quote. —Trans.)
84   *"those used against us"*: Marks, *The Search for the "Manchurian Candidate,"* 285–86.
84   *"of his Nazi complicity"*: Jacobsen, *Operation Paperclip,* 300.
85   *confided to his diary:* Ibid.
85   *over lunch: "pork chops":* Ibid., 301.
85   *"to make him talk"*: Müller, *Im Auftrag der Firma,* 453. Cf. Marks, 41.

17. LSD in America

86   *study of mental problems:* Lee and Shlain, *Acid Dreams,* 20.
87   *"interactions of cerebral processes"*: Dieter Hagenbach and Lucius Werthmüller, *Albert Hofmann und sein LSD* (Aarau and Munich: AT Verlag, 2011), 12. (The quote is taken from Stanislav Grof's forward, written originally in English and translated by Hagenbach and Werthmüller for their edition; the passage quoted here has been translated from German and is not a verbatim rendering. —Trans.)
87   *"her or his work"*: Hofmann, *LSD, My Problem Child,* 46.
89   *Stoll stated with satisfaction:* Arthur Stoll, "35 Jahre Mutterkornforschung und industrielle Mutterkornverwertung, Referat in der Sitzung vom 5.3.1953 des Verwaltungsrates der Sandoz AG Basel," Novartis Company Archive: C 102.001 (1953–54), 4.
90   *during the Nuremberg trials:* Arthur R. Turner (Chief Medical Intelligence Branch, War Department) to Henry K. Beecher, 7 February 1947: "Inclosed [*sic*] for your retention is a brochure, dealing with the Dachau Concentration Camp, which has just arrived. I . . . thought it might be of interest to you." Cf. McCoy, "Science in Dachau's Shadow," 410.

90 *"at deliberately suppressed information"*: Henry K. Beecher to Colonel Stone (Department of the Army) 15 June 1950, and Beecher to Surgeon General, 20 October 1951, Harvard Medical Library in the Francis A. Countway Library of Medicine, H MS c64, Box 11; the following two quotes as well.

91 *"for the Communist manipulator"*: Marks, Search for the "Manchurian Candidate," 134. By the end of the war 70 percent of the 7,190 American prisoners of war had made confessions or signed petitions that demanded that the US stop its war efforts in Asia. Fifteen percent cooperated fully with the Chinese, 5 percent resisted. Many of the former prisoners who returned home to America stood by their statements.

92 *the order of society*: Reeves, *Life and Times of Joe McCarthy*, 129.

92 *"necessary experimental animal, man"*: Lasagna, von Felsinger, and Beecher, "Drug-Induced Mood Changes in Man." Cf. "Medizin und Hygiene," No. 637, April 1964: "The ideal experimental animal is man. Whenever possible, one should use man as the experimental animal. The scientific researcher should keep the fact in mind that if he wants to study the diseases of man, he must study man. No studies are more interesting, more satisfying, and more lucrative than those that are carried out on man."

92 *the US Defense Department*: McCoy, 410.

93 *"weren't informed about anything"*: Müller, *Im Auftrag der Firma*, 318. Cf. James P. Rathwell, "Questionable LSD Experiments Lurk in Bioethics Icon's Background," Statnews.com, 16 June 2016, https://www.statnews.com/2016/06/16/bioethics-lsd-henry-knowles-beecher, and McCoy, 413. McCoy is also the source for the five following quotes.

93 *Research and Development Board*: Mashour, "Altered States," 4–11. In practice what this moratorium on publication does more than anything is to protect Beecher's reputation and prevent a realistic assessment of his work at the elite American university, which still holds him in high esteem, honoring him every year with the Beecher Prize, endowed with a $1,500 stipend and awarded to the student who writes the best essay on the topic of, of all things, medical ethics.

93 *"importance in New York"*: Ralph Paul Bircher to Albert Hofmann, 30 October 1952, FA Novartis: M370.010c 1942–52; the following quote as well.

93 *"account of trademark protection"*: Albert Hofmann to Ralph Paul Bircher, 12 December 1952, FA Novartis: M370.010c 1942–52. The subject of naming wasn't an easy one. Even the category of substance into which LSD was to be fit—and to which for example mescaline also

belonged—still didn't have an overarching designation (see Müller, 458). Some scientists called these drugs *phantastica*, others *psychotica*, which had less of a positive ring to it. In psychiatric circles the descriptor *psychotomimetics* was still in use, but did the drug really induce imitation psychoses? *Hallucinogens* was also floating around as a category, but it had a negative aftertaste—who would willingly want to start hallucinating? Another suggestion was *ataraxica*, which referred to the ideal of tranquility and to a condition of equanimity and calm in the face of misfortune. Yet another was *eidetics*, bringing forth ideas, or also *oneirogens*, producing dreams, or *entheogens*, which meant essentially *awakening the divine*. None of these neologisms gained currency, nor did *phrenotopica*, *neurotropica*, or *psychotropic drugs*. New names were constantly being proposed from this or that corner of the debate, and were rejected just as quickly: efforts that make it apparent just how much experts were groping in the dark when it came to pinning down what LSD really was—how difficult it was shaping up to be to find the means of capturing in language an extra-linguistic experience.

18. Brain Warfare

94 *program luridly put it:* Albarelli, *A Terrible Mistake,* 273.
94 *"impulses implanted from without":* Kinzer, *Poisoner in Chief,* 72. Cf. Müller, *Im Auftrag der Firma,* 341 and 399; the following two quotes as well. The full text of Dulles's speech is available online through the CIA website's FOIA reading room.
95 *code name was MK-Ultra:* The CIA cryptonym is a composite of the digraph *MK*, which refers to the program's origins in the agency's Technical Services Staff, and the word *Ultra*, which was used during the Second World War for the classification of sensitive materials.

19. CEO and CIA

96 *of his poor neighborhood:* Kinzer, *Poisoner in Chief,* 5.
96 *"hampered in my performance":* Ibid., 8.
97 *research data, and funds:* Cf. Müller, *Im Auftrag der Firma,* 29–30.
97 *"beyond those of alcohol":* Report, Beecher to the Surgeon General, 20 October 1951, Harvard Medical Library in the Francis A. Countway Library of Medicine, H MS c64, 2. Cf. McCoy, "Science in Dachau's Shadow," 411, as well as Müller, 324, and Koch and Wech, *Deckname Artischocke,* 299, n. 48.

97   *"many hours or days"*: Henry K. Beecher, "Information from Europe Related to the Ego-Depressants, 6 August to 29 August 1952," Harvard Medical Library in the Francis A. Countway Library of Medicine, H MS c64; the following two quotes as well.

98   *"development will look like"*: Carlo Henze to Albert Hofmann, 14 May 1953, Novartis Company Archive: M370.010c.

98   *agents on a plane*: Marks, *The Search for the "Manchurian Candidate,"* 71.

98   *came from Eastern Europe*: Lee and Shlain, *Acid Dreams,* 27. Cf. Müller, 592.

98   *"the very strictest confidence"*: Marks, 71. My inquiry at the Novartis archive met with the following response: "These two meetings in December 1953 have left behind no traces in our Sandoz materials" (Florence Wickler to the author, 16 July 2020, email from Novartis Company Archive).

99   *"first experienced it myself"*: Albarelli, *A Terrible Mistake,* 225.

99   *"me for several hours"*: Ibid., 226.

99   *'brotherhood of man'*: Barber, *Psychedelic Revolutionaries,* 276. Cf. Marks, 75. The following quotes here as well.

100 *evil things hidden everywhere*: Marks, 77.

100 *"became an occupational hazard"*: Marks, 76.

20. The Case of Frank Olson

102 *than he should have*: Marks, *The Search for the "Manchurian Candidate,"* 84ff.; the following quotes as well.

103 *"deep breath and died"*: Cf. Albarelli, *A Terrible Mistake,* 19.

21. Menticide

104 *"visible from the outside"*: Müller, *Im Auftrag der Firma,* 342.

104 *a comprehensive research program*: Ibid., 400. Cf. Marks, *The Search for the "Manchurian Candidate,"* 162.

105 *to him remained hidden*: Müller, 401.

105 *name of their patron*: Ibid., 482.

105 *discomfiture, or producing dependencies*: Ibid., 401; cf. 503 for the range of different projects.

106 *no one could match*: Cf. Müller, 458ff.

106 *Dulles, described these activities*: Jacobsen, *Operation Paperclip,* 366.

106 *of their strange behavior*: Marks, 110.

107 *"even know we existed"*: Barber, *Psychedelic Revolutionaries,* 278.

107   *"it better than you":* Müller, 613ff.; the following quote as well.
108   *interesting to the CIA:* Kinzer, *Poisoner in Chief,* 137.
109   *offenses at five years:* "Playboy Panel: The Drug Revolution," *Playboy Magazine* 17, no. 2 (February 1970): 58.
110   *in those days:* Marks, 69.
110   *the MK-Ultra chief:* Ibid, 68.
110   *clutches at age nineteen:* Ibid.

22. Operation Midnight Climax

112   *"[made] bathroom facilities essential":* Albarelli, *A Terrible Mistake,* 228.
114   *goal of the operation:* George Hunter White, Notebook entry from 16 September 1953, Stanford University Libraries: Dept. of Special Collections, George White Papers, M1111, Box 7, "Series 5. Notebooks and Diaries."
114   *"finding nobody really satisfactory":* Albarelli, 252.
114   *"liquids, and loose solids":* Ibid., 254.
114   *"of Deception for Women":* Melton and Wallace, *The Official C.I.A. Manual,* v.
115   *a CIA memorandum stated:* Albarelli, 185 and 229.
115   *"being tortured and whipped":* John Jacobs, "The Diaries of a CIA Operative," *Washington Post,* 5 September 1977. Cf. Marks, *The Search for the "Manchurian Candidate,"* 101.
115   *his bone-dry bureaucratese:* Marks, 101 and 106.
116   *"the funds were spent":* Ibid., 107.
116   *"important, like state secrets":* Ibid., 102.
117   *"career or anything else":* Ibid., 103–4.
117   *"can lead him gently":* Ibid, 103. Another safe house was set up in California in Marin County, just outside of San Francisco on the other side of the Golden Gate Bridge. While "the pad" was also suitable for quickies after lunch, the new safe house was used for experiments that required more isolation. Outside of the city, Gottlieb had stink bombs tested and tried out itching and sneezing powder as well as laxatives, so-called harassment substances.
117   *"of the All-Highest":* Marks, 109. The agents soon went to work outside the pad as well. They penetrated the scene in the Californian city and began dosing people with LSD on the street or in bars. Other drugs that the CIA wanted to test for foreign operations were also sent to the West Coast, for example BZ, which triggers violent behavior and hallucinations that can last for up to a week.
117   *"nature in the bedroom":* Marks, 103.

23. Mösch-Rümms

122   *and "air secrets"*: Bächi, *LSD auf dem Land,* 153.

123   *native tongue of Mixeteco:* These were captured on tape and can still be found online.

123   *of the camera's flash:* Bächi, 217.

123   *"board of an architect"*: Gordon Wasson, "Seeking the Magic Mushroom," *Life,* 13 May 1957, 102–20; all quotes in this description as well.

123   *"mushrooms are beyond belief"*: Bächi, 203–4.

123   *"took on real meaning"*: Wasson, 104.

123   *"struck us at once"*: Ibid., 102.

124   *"have been a secret"*: Ibid., 101. Cf. Bächi, 153.

124   *"coping with psychic disturbances"*: Wasson, 120.

124   *"total of 2.4 grams"*: "Aktennotiz einer Besprechung mit Prof. R. Heim, Músee d'Histoire Naturelle, Paris," 9 November 1956, Hofmann Papers, Box 135, 426; Hofmann, *LSD, My Problem Child,* 83.

124   *"on a Mexican character"*: Albert Hofmann to Ernst Jünger, 11 July 1957, Hofmann Papers, Box 136; Bächi, 248. The following three quotes as well.

125   *"to lysergic acid diethylamide"*: Albert Hofmann to Ernst Jünger, 11 July 1957.

126   *"nor reliably verified"*: "Aktennotiz einer Besprechung mit Prof. R. Heim"; "Besprechung mit Herrn Prof. R. Heim, Paris, über Züchtung und Untersuchung von mexikanischen Rauschpilzen," 28 March 1957, Hofmann Papers, Box 135, 557.

126   *his mentor, the centaur Chiron:* Thomas Pynchon mentions this window in his novel *Gravity's Rainbow.*

126   *Hofmann wrote proudly:* Hofmann, *LSD, My Problem Child,* 87.

126   *"and chemical-pharmacological research"*: Aurelio Cerletti, "Teonanacatl und Psilocybin," *Deutsche Medizinische Wochenschrift,* no. 52, 25 December 1959, 2318.

126   *hysteria, addiction, and depression:* Bächi, 232.

127   *and made it respectable:* Ibid.

127   *"things yet to yield"*: Albert Hofmann, Memo, Novartis Company Archive: H-105.022 (1953–57), 7; the following quotes as well.

24. Bulk Order

129   *"a pinch of psychedelic"*: Cited in "Humphry Osmond," obituary. Cf. Pollan, *How to Change Your Mind,* 163.

129   *"self-acceptance and self-understanding"*: Barber, *Psychedelic Revolutionaries,* 288.

130   *"wanted until this treatment"*: Lee and Shlain, *Acid Dreams,* 57.
130   *"politicians should take it"*: Fuchs, "Alles so bunt hier." (Quote trans-
      lated from Fuchs's German; not a verbatim rendering of the source
      quote. —Trans.)
130   *"The CIA work stinks"*: Lee and Shlain, 52.
130   *"L.S.D., 25 ampoules per box"*: P. Hartmann (Sandoz Pharmaceuticals,
      Hanover, New Jersey) to Dr. A. M. Hubbard, Uranium Corp. of B.C.
      Ltd., 31 May 1955, New Westminster Archives. Cf. Albarelli, *A Terrible
      Mistake,* 239.
130   *then see what happens:* Lee and Shlain, 53.
131   *"body, outside my mind"*: Ibid., 73, 77; the following quote as well.
131   *"The cure is biochemical"*: Ibid., 77–79; the following quote as well.
132   *"world with this stuff"*: Ibid., 80.
132   *Americans on a trip:* Leary to L. Light and Co., 30 December 1962,
      and Leary to Hoffmann-La Roche, 11 January 1963, Hofmann Papers,
      Box 136 (Leary). On his Harvard letterhead Leary also asked for the
      availability and price of DMT, DET, Hydroxy-DMT, and bufotenin:
      substances containing dimethyltryptamine, which causes extremely
      strong hallucinations.
132   *"as the Ford Foundation"*: L. Light and Company LTD to Timothy Leary,
      8 January 1963, Hofmann Papers, Box 136 (Leary); the following quote
      as well.
133   *came back to bite him:* Lee and Shlain, 85. "Information concerning the
      use of this kind of drugs for experimental and personal reasons should
      be reported immediately."
133   *"CAUTION"*: Timothy Leary to the director of the L. Light and Com-
      pany, LTD, 22 January 1963, Hofmann Papers: Box 136 (Leary).
133   *"appreciable amounts"*: Albert Hofmann to Timothy Leary, 24 January
      1963, Hofmann Papers, Box 136 (Leary); the following two quotes as
      well. Hofmann had sent a letter to Leary two years earlier in which he
      praised the professor for using psilocybin as a "consciousness expanding
      drug," as well as for having understood the importance of "settings"—
      that is, the location and the conditions—for an enriching experience, a
      point that many psychiatrists "don't pay due attention to at this point."
      (Albert Hofmann to Timothy Leary, 22 February 1961, Box 136 [Leary]).
133   *"within about 3–4 weeks"*: Sandoz LTD to Leary, 24 January 1963,
      Hofmann Papers: Box 136 (Leary); the following two quotes as well.
133   *"necessary explanations"*: "Telephongespräch mit Herrn Mason," 29
      January 1963, Hofmann Papers, box 136 (Leary).
134   *"dealing with LSD and psilocybin"*: Carlo Henze to Yves Dunant, 7 Febru-
      ary 1963, Hofmann Papers, box 136 (Leary); the following quote as well.

134 *"the many files"*: FDA to Carlo Henze, 31 January 1963, Hofmann Papers, Box 136 (Leary).

134 *"slate was clean"*: Carlo Henze to Yves Dunant, 7 February 1963. The following quotes here as well.

135 *should they visit the United States:* Within the company there were objections to Henze's view of things. The Sandoz employee Ch. Grisel, who put together a chronology of the events, pointed to the fact that the sales quote sent to Leary had included a clause requesting the "import license issued by your competent authorities according to the new regulations referring to such drugs." As a result, Grisel didn't believe that the organization's reputation with the FDA would suffer: "The promise to this authority has not been broken, since we've said that we'll only deliver if the FDA gives its approval. I believe that we've gone to more trouble here to cater to the FDA than might actually be appreciated by this authority." (Grisel, Ch. "Harward [*sic*] University, Cambridge (Mass.), LSD/Psilocybin–Brief Dr. Henze vom 7.2.63," Novartis Company Archive: H-124.002.)

135 *complied with the request:* Sandoz, Ltd. to Franklin L. Ford, Dean of the Faculty of Arts and Sciences, Harward [*sic*] University, 5 February 1963, Hofmann Papers, Box 136 (Leary).

135 *"ever be supplied"*: Renz and Albert Hofmann to Laszlo, 6 February 1963, Hofmann Papers, Box 136 (Leary).

135 *"What does that mean?"*: Timothy Leary to Albert Hofmann, 13 February 1963, with Hofmann's handwritten comments, Hofmann Papers, Box 136 (Leary).

136 *"Apparently that's the most important thing!"*: Albert Hofmann to Timothy Leary, 22 February 1963.

136 *his opinion of Leary:* Albert Hofmann to Aldous Huxley, 11 March 1963.

136 *"annoyed & disturbed"*: Aldous Huxley to Albert Hofmann, 24 February 1962 and 21 March 1963; the following two quotes as well.

136 *"accept this order"*: Sandoz Ltd. to Timothy Leary, 26 February 1963. Cf. Sandoz Ltd. to Timothy Leary, 19 March 1963.

137 *"A windbag"*: Henze, handwritten letter, 31 May 1996.

137 *for months after use:* Herbert Black, "Monsters and Murder Are So Real with LSD," *Boston Globe*, 26 September 1965. Cf. Nancy H. Davis, "Physician Says Harvard Students Have Suffered from LSD Effects," *Harvard Crimson*, 28 September 1965.

137 *"people who have NOT taken it"*: http://allauthor.com/quotes/173997

137 *"several hundred orgasms"*: Bernard Gavzer, "The Playboy Interview with Timothy Leary," *Playboy*, September 1966.

137 *"We've stirred up enough trouble"*: Leary, *Flashbacks,* 114.

138   *"making [their] work far harder":* Barber, 274.

138   *"he went overboard":* Lee and Shlain, 88.

138   *"genuinely concerned":* Barber, 267. Sidney Gottlieb kept a sharp eye on the mounting controversy surrounding the rebellious professor. Leary was one of the few researchers whose findings didn't automatically land on his desk. For that reason he had already inserted an informant into the orbit of the promiscuous LSD prophet. As one CIA memo put it, "Uncontrolled experimentation has in the past resulted in tragic circumstances and for this reason every effort is made to control any involvement with these drugs" (Lee and Shlain, 85).

25. LSDJFK

139   *"Amused, arrogant, aristocratic":* Leary, *Flashbacks,* 128–29; the following quotes in this passage as well.

140   *"part of the furniture":* Burleigh, *A Very Private Woman,* 194.

140   *"as big as he wants":* John F. Kennedy, "Commencement Address at American University," 10 June 1963, available online at https://www.jfklibrary.org/archives/other-resources/john-f-kennedy-speeches/american-university-19630610; the following quote as well.

26. The Revolt of the Guinea Pigs

141   *"spreading infection":* "An Editorial," *Harvard Crimson,* 28 May 1963.

141   *"more important than Harvard":* "Psychic Research. LSD—And All That," *Time,* March 29, 1963.

142   *"Girl, 5, Eats LSD":* Lee and Shlain, *Acid Dreams,* 150.

142   *"not so crazy after all":* Ibid., 119.

142   *"the revolt of the guinea pigs":* Pollan, *How to Change Your Mind,* 206.

143   *"give us freedom":* The Beatles Anthology (San Francisco: Chronicle Books, 2000), 179. See also Hagenbach and Werthmüller, *Albert Hofmann und sein LSD,* 192.

143   *"a big submarine":* Legs McNeil and Gillian McCain, "The Oral History of the First Two Times the Beatles Took Acid," *Vice,* 4 December 2016, https://www.vice.com/en/article/ppawq9/the-oral-history-of-the-beatles-first-two-acids-trips-legs-mcneil-gillian-mccain.

143   *"break barriers":* Mikal Gilmore, "Beatles' Acid Test: How LSD Opened the Door to 'Revolver,'" *Rolling Stone,* 25 August 2016, https://www.rollingstone.com/feature/beatles-acid-test-how-lsd-opened-the-door-to-revolver-251417.

144 *"no spiritual sustenance"*: "Playboy Panel: The Drug Revolution," *Playboy* 17, no. 2 (February 1970).

144 *"Flush their drug kicks"*: Burroughs, *Nova Express*, 6.

144 *"The whole 'mind expansion' hype"*: Barber, *Psychedelic Revolutionaries*, 280.

145 *"to protect the public health"*: "Drug Abuse Control Amendments," 15 July 1965, https://catalog.archives.gov/id/299906.

145 *"including Switzerland"*: Sandoz A.G. Press Release, Division of Publicity, 18 April 1966, Hofmann Papers, 148.6a.

145 *refrigerator that was chained shut*: Barber, 273.

28. Elvis Meets Nixon

148 *"health, vitality, and self-respect"*: Lyndon B. Johnson, "Special Message to the Congress on Crime and Law Enforcement: 'To Insure the Public Safety,'" 7 February 1968, *Public Papers of the Presidents of the United States: Lyndon B. Johnson (1968, Book 1)* (Washington: United States Government Printing Office, 1970).

149 *"When the president does it"*: Müller, *Im Auftrag der Firma*, 697.

149 *"The Nixon campaign"*: Dan Baum, "Legalize It All," *Harper's Magazine*, April 2016, 22.

149 *"admire[d]" president*: Elvis Presley to Richard Nixon, undated, handwritten, National Security Archives, "The Nixon-Presley Meeting, 21 December 1970"; the following seven quotes as well.

151 *"If the President wants to meet"*: Dwight L. Chapin to H.R. Haldeman, Memorandum, 21 December 1970, https://www.archives.gov/exhibits/nixon-met-elvis/page-5.html.

151 *"anti-American spirit"*: Bud Krogh, "Meeting with Elvis Presley, Monday, December 21, 1970, 12:30 p.m.," Memorandum and Bud Krogh to Neal Ball, "Guidance on Jack Anderson Column–Elvis Presley," Memorandum 27 January 1972, https://www.archives.gov/exhibits/nixon-met-elvis/page-5.html The following quote and quotes from the dialogue as well.

153 *"the average American family"*: Memorandum for the President, "Meeting with Elvis Presley, December 21, 1970, 12:30 p.m."

153 *"something we can pursue"*: Ibid.

153 *"I'm really a big supporter"*: Krogh, "Meeting with Elvis Presley."

29. A Case of Wine

155 *"current total level"*: Sandoz A.G. Direktionskomittee to Albert Hofmann, undated, Private Collection.

155   *"honorarium taking into account":* Ibid.

156   *Hofmann was to learn:* The downplaying of Hofmann's achievements had begun much earlier. It is of note that Arthur Stoll often put his own name first when Hofmann developed a new medication or published a new study. As a staffer in a leading position at Novartis told the author in conversation, "That isn't done. The lead scientist is always named first. And that would have been Hofmann." (Frank Petersen, conversation with author, 24 March 2022, Novartis Campus, Basel, Switzerland.)

156   *Those at the top:* Cf. Albert Hofmann to Dr. Ian Collins, 17 March 1964, Hofmann Papers, 135 (Heim), 168. As late as 1964, for example, Hofmann was still studying mushrooms from Papua New Guinea.

156   *"As we have informed you":* C. M. Jacottet to Albert Hofmann, 21 July 1967, private collection.

156   *"brilliant business":* Albert Hofmann to Marc Moret, Vice President and Delegate of the Administrative Council, 7 May 1985, private collection.

156   *"This is made in recognition":* Sandoz A.G. Direktion to Albert Hofmann, 5 November 1987, private collection.

157   *In more recent years:* "Keine Zutaten mehr aus der Schweiz für Todesspritzen," *Handelszeitung,* 9 September 2013.

30. Light Vader Hofmann

158   *"The history of LSD":* Hofmann, *LSD, My Problem Child,* 5.

160   *"Mysteries played":* Hagenbach and Werthmüller, *Albert Hofmann und sein LSD,* 309.

160   *"Instead of visiting":* Albert Hofmann to Dr. Humphry Osmond, 27 September 1973, Hofmann Papers, Box 136, 1.

161   *"As you are no doubt aware":* Pascal Couchepin (Chairman of the Swiss Department of the Interior [EDI]) to Dieter A. Hagenbach (President, Gaia Media Foundation), 7 April 2006, private collection.

161   *Also in 2007:* Rachel Williams, "Sheer Genius: From the Web to Homer Simpson," *Guardian,* 29 October 2007, https://www.theguardian.com/uk/2007/oct/29/artnews.art.

Epilogue: LSD for Mom

164   *"The receptors are like keyholes":* Franz Vollenweider, conversation with the author, 25 March 2022, University of Zurich Psychiatric Hospital; all of the following quotes in this conversation as well.

168   *"dedicates its efforts"*: DZNE website, https://www.dzne.de/en/about
      -us/uebersicht; accessed 17 February 2023.

168   *"background conversation"*: DZNE Stabstelle Kommunikation to the
      author, email, 3 May 2022; the following quote as well.

168   *"to find novel approaches"*: DZNE website.

168   *"susceptible to charlatanism"*: Alzheimer's expert (name withheld),
      phone interview with author, 17 May 2022.

176   *"In our Western civilization"*: Albert Hofmann to Aldous Huxley, 11
      March 1963, Hofmann Papers.

BIBLIOGRAPHY

The most important sources for this book were unpublished documents from the following archives in Switzerland, the United States, Canada, Germany, and Great Britain: the Novartis Company Archive, the Archive of the Eidgenössische Technische Hochschule Zürich (ETH), the Archive of the Universität Bern (Hofmann Papers), the Schweizerisches Kunstarchiv Zürich, the Archive of the Max Planck Society, the Harvard Medical Library in the Francis A. Countway Library of Medicine, Stanford University Libraries, the United States' National Archives and Records Administration (NARA), the National Security Archives, the University Archives of Penn State University, the National Archives of Great Britain, and the New Westminster Archives, Canada.

Works Cited

Albarelli, H. P., Jr. *A Terrible Mistake: The Murder of Frank Olson and the CIA's Secret Cold War Experiments*. Waterville, Oregon: Trine Day, 2009.

Bächi, Beat. *LSD auf dem Land: Produktion und kollektive Wirkung psychotroper Stoffe*. Konstanz, Germany: Konstanz University Press, 2020.

Barber, P. W. *Psychedelic Revolutionaries: Three Medical Pioneers, the Fall of Hallucinogenic Research, and the Rise of Big Pharma*. Regina, Saskatchewan: University of Regina Press, 2018.

Bauer, Veit Harold. *Das Antonius-Feuer in Kunst und Medizin*. Berlin: Sandoz, 1973.

Beringer, Kurt. *Der Meskalinrausch, Seine Geschichte und Erscheinungsweise*. Berlin: Springer, 1927.

Brüschweiler, Jura, Hansjakop Diggelmann, and Hans A. Lüthy. *Sammlung Arthur Stoll: Skulpturen und Gemälden des 19. und 20. Jahrhunderts*. Introduction by Marcel Fischer. Zurich: SIK-ISEA, 1961.

Burleigh, Nina. *A Very Private Woman: The Life and Unsolved Murder of Presidential Mistress Mary Meyer*. New York: Bantam Books, 1998.

Burroughs, William. *Nova Express*. New York: Grove, 1964.

Collins, John. *Legalising the Drug Wars: A Regulatory History of UN Drug Control*. Cambridge: Cambridge University Press, 2022.

Deichmann, Ute. *Flüchten, Mitmachen, Vergessen: Chemiker und Biochemiker in der NS-Zeit*. Weinheim, Germany: Wiley VCH, 2001.

Fry, Helen. *The London Cage: The Secret History of Britain's World War II Interrogation Center*. New Haven: Yale University Press, 2017.

Fuchs, Oliver. "Alles so bunt hier." *Süddeutsche Zeitung*. May 17, 2010.

Goudsmit, Samuel A. *Alsos*. New York: Schuman, 1947.

Hagenbach, Dieter, and Lucius Werthmüller. *Albert Hofmann und sein LSD*. Aarau, Switzerland: AT Verlag, 2011.

Henze, Carlo. "Recollections of a Medical Intelligence Officer in World War II." *Bulletin of the New York Academy of Medicine* 49, no. 11 (Nov. 1973).

Herer, Jack. *Hemp and the Marijuana Conspiracy: The Emperor Wears No Clothes*. Van Nuys, California: Hemp Publishing, 1995.

Hofmann, Albert. *LSD, My Problem Child and Insights/Outlooks*. Trans. Jonathan Ott. Oxford: Beckley Foundation Press and Oxford University Press, 2013.

Holzer, Tilmann. *Die Geburt der Drogenpolitik aus dem Geist der Rassenhygiene: Deutsche Drogenpolitik von 1933 bis 1972*. Norderstedt, Germany: Books on Demand, 2007.

"Humphry Osmond." Obituary. *BMJ* 328 (2004): 713.

Independent Commission of Experts Switzerland. *Switzerland, National Socialism, and the Second World War: Final Report*. Zurich: Pendo Verlag, 2002.

Jacobsen, Annie. *Operation Paperclip: The Secret Intelligence Program That Brought Nazi Scientists to America*. New York: Little, Brown, 2014.

Jähner, Harald. *Aftermath: Life in the Fallout of the Third Reich, 1945–1955*. Trans. Shaun Whiteside. New York: Knopf, 2022.

Kinzer, Stephen. *Poisoner in Chief: Sidney Gottlieb and the Search for Mind Control*. New York: Henry Holt, 2019.

Koch, Egmont R., and Michael Wech. *Deckname Artischocke: Die geheimen Menschenversuche der CIA*. Munich: C. Bertelsmann, 2002.

Kopp, Manfred. "Lesen wie in einem offenen Buch: US Military Intelligence Group, 1946–1968." *Sonderdruck aus dem Jahrbuch des Hochtaunuskreis 2011*. Oberursel, Germany, 2011.

Lasagna, Louis, John M. von Felsinger, and Henry K. Beecher. "Drug-Induced Mood Changes in Man. 1. Observations on Healthy Subjects, Chronically Ill Patients, and 'Postaddicts,'" *Journal of the American Medical Association* 157, no. 12 (March 19, 1955). DOI: 10.1001/jama.1955.02950290026009.

Leary, Timothy. *Flashbacks: An Autobiography*. Los Angeles: Jeremy P. Tarcher, 1990.

Lee, Martin A., and Bruce Shlain. *Acid Dreams: The Complete Social History of LSD: The CIA, the Sixties, and Beyond*. New York: Grove, 1985.

Marks, John. *The Search for the "Manchurian Candidate": The CIA and Mind Control: The Secret History of the Behavioral Sciences*. New York: Norton, 1991.

Mashour, George A. "Altered States: LSD and the Anesthesia Laboratory of Henry Knowles Beecher." *Bulletin of Anesthesia History* 23, no. 3 (July 2005). Doi: 10.1016/s1522–8649(05)50033-7.

McCoy, Alfred. "Science in Dachau's Shadow: Hebb, Beecher, and the Development of CIA Psychological Torture and Modern Medical Ethics." *Journal of the History of the Behavioral Sciences* 43, no. 4 (Fall 2007).

McWilliams, John C. *The Protectors: Harry J. Anslinger and the Federal Bureau of Narcotics, 1930–1962*. Newark: University of Delaware Press, 1990.

Melton, Keith H., and Robert Wallace. *The Official C.I.A. Manual of Trickery and Deception*. New York: William Morrow, 2010.

Moser, Jeannie. "Psychotropes Wissen: Figuren und Narrative im drogistischen Selbst-Experiment." Doctoral thesis, University of Vienna, 2010, https://services.phaidra.univie.ac.at/api/object/o:1274059/get.

Müller, Knuth. *Im Auftrag der Firma: Geschichte und Folgen einer unerwarteten Liaison zwischen Psychoanalyse und militärisch-geheimdienstlichen Netzwerken der USA seit 1940*. Giessen, Germany: Psychosozial-Verlag, 2017.

Nasher, Jack. *Entlarvt! Wie Sie in jedem Gespräch an die ganze Wahrheit kommen*. Frankfurt: Campus Verlag, 2015.

Newton, David E. *Marijuana: A Reference Handbook*. Santa Barbara, California: ABC-CLIO, 2017.

Ohler, Norman. *Der totale Rausch*. Cologne, Germany: Kiepenheuer and Witsch, 2015.

Pickard, Leonard. *The Rose of Paracelsus: On Secrets and Sacraments*. San Bernadino, California: Sub Rosa Press, 2016.

Pollan, Michael. *How to Change Your Mind: What the New Science of Psychedelics Teaches Us about Consciousness, Dying, Addiction, Depression, and Transcendence*. New York: Penguin Press, 2018.

Raz, Shlomi. "Lysergic Acid Diethylamide as a Prospective Multi-Target Disease Modifying Therapeutic in Alzheimer's Disease." White Paper, Eleusis Therapeutics Ltd., 2020.

Reeves, Richard. *Daring Young Men: The Heroism and Triumph of the Berlin Airlift, June 1948–May 1949.* New York: Simon & Schuster, 2010.

Reeves, Thomas C. *The Life and Times of Senator Joe McCarthy.* Briarcliff Manor, New York: Stein and Day, 1982.

Reitzenstein, Julien. *Himmlers Forscher. Wehrwissenschaft und Medizinverbrechen im "Ahnenerbe" der SS.* Paderborn, Germany: Ferdinand Schöningh, 2014.

Schmaltz, Florian. *Kampfstoff-Forschung im Nazionalsozialismus: Zur Kooperation von Kaiser-Wilhelm-Instituten, Militär und Industrie.* Göttingen, Germany: Wallstein, 2005.

Schmersahl, Peter. "Mutterkorn: Halluzinogen und Auslöser von Vergiftungen." *Deutsche Apotheker Zeitung,* no. 29 (July 22, 2010).

"Stanislav Grof Interviews Dr. Albert Hofmann—Esalen Institute, Big Sur, California, 1984." *Maps* 11, no. 2 (fall 2001).

Stoll, Werner. "Lysergsäure-diäthylamid, ein Phantastikum aus der Mutterkorngruppe." *Schweizer Archiv für Neurologie und Psychiatrie.* 1947.

Trials of War Criminals Before the Nuremberg Military Tribunals Under Control Council Law no. 10, vol. 2. Washington, DC: US Government Printing Office, 1949.

Willstätter, Richard. *Aus meinem Leben.* Weinheim, Germany: Verlag-Chemie, 1949.

Further Reading

Bernadac, Christian. *Devil's Doctors: Medical Experiments on Human Subjects in the Concentration Camps.* Geneva: Ferni Publishing House, 1978.

Blackman, Shane. *Chilling Out: The Cultural Politics of Substance Consumption, Youth and Drug Policy.* Maidenhead, England: Open University Press, 2004.

Bobrenjow, Wladimir, and Waleri Rjasanzew. *Das Geheimlabor des KGB: Gespenster der Warsonowjew-Gasse.* Berlin: Edition q, 1993.

Bredekamp, Horst. *The Lure of Antiquity and the Cult of the Machine: The Kunstkammer and the Evolution of Nature, Art, and Technology.* Princeton: Markus Wiener Publishers, 1995.

Briesen, Detlef. *Drogenkonsum und Drogenpolitik in Deutschland und den USA: Ein historischer Vergleich.* Frankfurt: Campus, 2005.

Burroughs, William. *Naked Lunch.* New York: Grove, 2009.

Campbell, Nancy D., J. P. Olsen, and Luke Walden. *The Narcotic Farm: The*

Rise and Fall of America's First Prison for Drug Addicts. Lexington, Kentucky: Limestone Books, 2021.

Courtwright, David T. *Forces of Habit: Drugs and the Making of the Modern World.* Cambridge: Harvard University Press, 2002.

Davenport-Hines, Richard. *The Pursuit of Oblivion: A Social History of Narcotics.* New York: Norton, 2001.

Davis, Erik. *High Weirdness: Drugs, Esoterica, and Visionary Experience in the Seventies.* Cambridge: MIT Press, 2019.

Davis, Steven L., and Bill Minutaglio. *The Most Dangerous Man in America: Timothy Leary, Richard Nixon and the Hunt for the Fugitive King of LSD.* New York: Twelve, 2018.

DeJong, David. *Nazi Billionaires: The Dark History of Germany's Wealthiest Dynasties.* Boston: Mariner Books, 2022.

De Quincey, Thomas. *Confessions of an English Opium Eater and Other Writings.* London: Penguin, 2003.

Dyck, Joachim. *Der Zeitzeuge. Gottfried Benn 1929–1949.* Göttingen: Wallstein, 2006.

Erbacher, Felix. *Pioniere der Basler Wirtschaft.* Basel: Münsterverlag, 2014.

Fadiman, James. *The Psychedelic Explorer's Guide: Safe, Therapeutic, and Sacred Journeys.* Rochester, Vermont: Park Street Press, 2011.

Griffiths R. R., M. W. Johnson, M. A. Carducci, et al. "Psilocybin Produces Substantial and Sustained Decreases in Depression and Anxiety in Patients with Life-Threatening Cancer: A Randomized Double-Blind Trial." *Journal of Psychopharmacology* 30, no. 13 (2016): doi:10.1177/0269881116675513.

Hanske, Paul-Philipp, and Benedikt Sarreiter, eds. *Neues von der anderen Seite. Die Wiederentdeckung des Psychedelischen.* Berlin: Suhrkamp, 2015.

Hari, Johann. *Chasing the Scream: The First and Last Days of the War on Drugs.* New York: Bloomsbury, 2015.

Hart, Carl L. *Drug Use for Grown-Ups: Chasing Liberty in the Land of Fear.* New York: Penguin Press, 2021.

Hofmann, Albert, Carl A. P. Ruck, and Gordon Wasson. *The Road to Eleusis: Unveiling the Secret of the Mysteries.* Berkeley: North Atlantic Books, 2008.

Holiday, Billie, and William Dufty. *Lady Sings the Blues.* New York: Harlem Moon, 2006.

Huxley, Aldous. *Brave New World.* London: Random House, 2022.

Huxley, Aldous. Speech to the Tavistock Group, California Medical School. 1961.
———. *The Doors of Perception.* New York: Harper Perennial, 2009.

Iversen, Leslie. *Drogen und Medikamente.* Stuttgart, Germany: Reclam, 2004.

Janney, Peter. *Mary's Mosaic: The CIA Conspiracy to Murder John F. Kennedy, Mary Pinchot Meyer, and Their Vision for World Peace.* New York: Skyhorse, 2012.

Jarnow, Jesse. *Heads: A Biography of Psychedelic America*. Philadelphia: Da Capo Press, 2016.

Johnson, Lyndon B. "Special Message to the Congress on Crime and Law Enforcement: 'To Insure the Public Safety.'" February 7, 1968. *Public Papers of the Presidents of the United States: Lyndon B. Johnson (1968, Book 1)*. Washington: United States Government Printing Office, 1970.

Jünger, Ernst. *Annäherungen: Drogen und Rausch*. Stuttgart, Germany: Klett-Cotta, 2021.

Ka-Tzetnik. *Shivitti: A Vision*. Trans. by Eli-yah Nina De-Nur and Lisa Harman. San Francisco: Harper & Row, 1989.

Kennedy, John F. "Commencement Address at American University," Washington, DC. June 10, 1963.

Kerouac, Jack. *On the Road*. New York: Viking, 1957.

Kesey, Ken. *One Flew over the Cuckoo's Nest*. New York: Viking, 1962.

Kraepelin, Emil. "Über die Einwirkung einiger medikamentöser Stoffe auf die Dauer einfacher psychischer Vorgänge." 1883.

Kupfer, Alexander. *Göttliche Gifte*. Stuttgart, Germany: Verlag J. B. Metzler, 1966.

Leary, Timothy, Richard Alpert, and Ralph Metzner. *The Psychedelic Experience: A Manual Based on the Tibetan Book of the Dead*. New York: University Books, 1964.

Letcher, Andy. *Shroom: A Cultural History of the Magic Mushroom*. New York: Ecco, 2007.

Lewin, Louis. *Phantastica: Narcotic and Stimulating Drugs, Their Use and Abuse*. London: Paul, Trench, Trubner, 1931.

Lüthy, Hans A. *F. Hodler. Sechzehn Bilder aus der Sammlung Arthur Stoll*. Lucerne, Switzerland: Kunstkreis, 1968.

Marinković, Milena. "The Future of Psychedelics in Alzheimer's Disease Treatment," MIND Foundation website. June 11, 2021. https://mind-foundation.org/psychedelics-alzheimers-disease-treatment.

McKenna, Terence. *Food of the Gods: The Search for the Original Tree of Knowledge: A Radical History of Plants, Drugs, and Human Evolution*. New York: Bantam Books, 1993.

Meyer-Wehlack, Benno. *Schlattenschammes oder Berlin am Meer. Erzählung aus dem Nachkrieg*. Berlin: Verlag Das Arsenal, 2015.

Moser, Jeannie. *Psychotropen, eine LSD-Biographie*. Konstanz, Germany: Konstanz University Press, 2013.

Pickard, William Leonard. "International LSD Prevalence—Factors Affecting Proliferation and Control." Erowid website. https://erowid.org/culture/characters/pickard_leonard/pickard_leonard_article1.pdf.

Poulsson, Edvard. *Poulsson's Lehrbuch für Pharmakologie für Ärtze und Studierende*. Leipzig, Germany: Hirzel, 1944.

Pynchon, Thomas. *Gravity's Rainbow*. New York: Viking, 1973.

Reko, Viktor. *Magische Gifte: Rausch- und Betäubungsmittel der neuen Welt*. Stuttgart, Germany: 1938.

Roshani, Anuschka. *Gleißen—Wie mich LSD fürs Leben kurierte*. Zurich: Kein und Aber, 2022.

Schmidt, Ulf. *Secret Science: A Century of Poison Warfare and Human Experiments*. Oxford: Oxford University Press, 2015.

Sessa, Ben. *The Psychedelic Renaissance: Reassessing the Role of Psychedelic Drugs in Twenty-First Century Psychiatry and Society*. London: Muswell Hill Press, 2017.

Shulgin, Alexander T. and Ann. *Pihkal: A Chemical Love Story*. Berkeley: Transform Press, 1995.

Stoll, Arthur, and Richard Willstätter. "Untersuchungen über Chlorophyll." Berlin, 1913.

Streatfield, Dominic. *Brainwash: The Secret History of Mind Control*. New York: Thomas Dunne Books, 2007.

Szasz, Thomas S. *Ceremonial Chemistry: The Ritual Persecution of Drugs, Addicts, and Pushers*. Syracuse: Syracuse University Press, 2003.

Taylor, Kathleen. *Brainwashing: The Science of Thought Control*. Oxford: Oxford University Press, 2017.

Thompson, Hunter S. *Fear and Loathing in Las Vegas*. New York: Vintage, 1998.

Vannini, Claudio, and Maurizio Venturini. *Halluzinogene, Entwicklung der Forschung, 1938 bis in die Gegenwart, Schwerpunkt Schweiz*. Berlin: VWB, 1999.

Wade, Simeon. *Foucault in California: A True Story—Wherein the Great French Philosopher Drops Acid in the Valley of Death*. Berkeley: Heyday, 2019.

Waldman, Ayelet. *A Really Good Day: How Microdosing Made a Mega Difference in My Mood, My Marriage, and My Life*. New York: Knopf, 2017.

Wasson, Valentina Pavlovna and Gordon R. *Mushrooms, Russia, and History*. New York: Pantheon, 1957.

Wittmann, Marc. *Wenn die Zeit stehen bleibt. Wie Schrecksekunden, Nahtod-Erfahrungen, Drogen, Meditation uns an die Grenzen des Bewusstseins führen*. Munich: C. H. Beck, 2015.

Wolfe, Thomas. *The Electric Kool-Aid Acid Test*. New York: Picador, 2008.

IMAGE CREDITS

INDEX

Page numbers in *italics* refer to illustrations.